Study Companion

DRIVE RIGHT

ELEVENTH EDITION

authors

- Owen Crabb
- Randall R. Thiel
- Elizabeth A. Weaver
- Frederik R. Mottola

SAVVAS
LEARNING COMPANY

What is the *Drive Right Study Companion?*

The word *companion* means friend and helper. The *Drive Right Study Companion* is a friend and helper to the student who is studying *Drive Right* and who wants to learn how to drive. This book helps you understand *Drive Right*. It explains many of the words and ideas in the book.

How do I use the *Study Companion?*

The *Study Companion* is organized in the same way as *Drive Right*. The *Study Companion* has the same chapters as *Drive Right*. Each chapter in the *Study Companion* has the same sections as the chapter in *Drive Right*.

Read the section in the *Study Companion* before you read the same section in *Drive Right*. Each section in the *Study Companion* has a part titled "Words and Ideas." In this part, new words and ideas are explained. The words are explained in the order that they are found in *Drive Right*. You can also read the *Study Companion* while you are reading *Drive Right*.

Each chapter has some activities to help you learn the words and ideas. These activities are not tests. There are three types of activities. "Figure It Out" asks you to use information in the *Study Companion* or in *Drive Right* to answer some questions. "Double Trouble" helps you understand words that have two or more meanings. "Think About It" asks you to use what you know about driving and the world around you to answer the questions. The activities are multiple choice, true or false, and short answers.

At the end of the *Study Companion* is an index. The index has all the vocabulary words and ideas in the *Study Companion* in alphabetical order. You can use the index to find the meaning of a word. The number next to the word tells you the page where you can find the word in the *Study Companion*.

Savvas Learning Company LLC, 15 East Midland Avenue, Paramus, NJ 07652

SAVVAS
LEARNING COMPANY

ISBN-13: 978-0-13-361265-3
ISBN-10: 0-13-361265-1
10 2020

Contents

Unit 1: The Driving Task

Ch 1 You Are the Driver 5
2 Signs, Signals, and Roadway Markings 11
3 Basic Vehicle Operation 18
4 Performing Basic Vehicle Maneuvers 26

Unit 2: Being a Responsible Driver

Ch 5 Managing Risk with the IPDE Process 32
6 Effects of Driver Condition 41
7 Alcohol, Other Drugs, and Driving 46
8 Managing Distractions 51

Unit 3: Controlling Your Vehicle

Ch 9 Natural Laws and Car Control 54
10 Negotiating Intersections 63
11 Sharing the Roadway 70
12 Driving in Adverse Conditions 77
13 Handling Emergencies 82

Unit 4: Driving in Different Environments

Ch 14 Driving in City Traffic 89
15 Driving in Rural Areas 94
16 Driving on Highways 99
17 Buying and Maintaining a Vehicle 103
18 Planning Your Travel 107

Answer Key 109

Name ______________________ Date ____________

Learning New Words

Take a look at Chapter 1 to familiarize yourself with the topics covered. Look for all the highlighted words in **dark** print. These are the vocabulary words. Write the words on a sheet of paper, then write the meaning next to each word. If you don't know the meaning of the word, use the Glossary at the back of *Drive Right*. You can also learn the meaning of a word by looking it up in the Index at the back of *Drive Right* for the page numbers where the word first appears. Some words are explained in this *Study Companion*.

Chapter 1: You are the Driver
Vocabulary List
1. risk: The main risk in driving is the possibility of having a conflict that results in a collision.
2. highway transportation system (HTS): This is a complex system made up of people, vehicles, and roadways.
3. Vehicle code: These are federal and state laws that regulate the HTS.

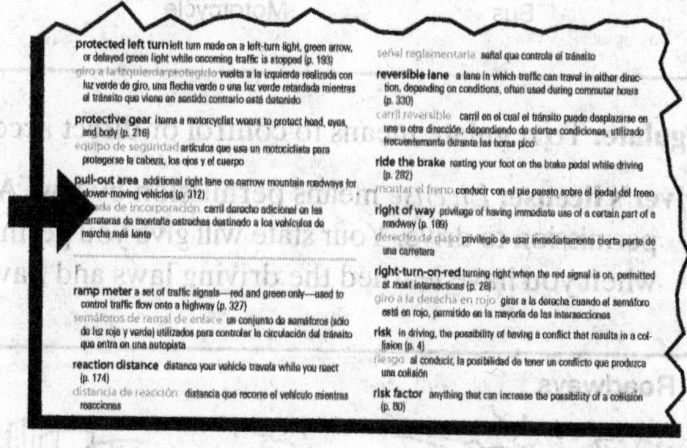

protected left turn left turn made on a left-turn light, green arrow, or delayed green light while oncoming traffic is stopped (p. 193)
giro a la izquierda protegido vuelta a la izquierda realizada con luz verde de giro, una flecha verde o una luz verde retardada mientras el tránsito que viene en sentido contrario está detenido

protective gear items a motorcyclist wears to protect head, eyes, and body (p. 216)
equipo de seguridad artículos que usa un motociclista para protegerse la cabeza, los ojos y el cuerpo

pull-out area additional right lane on narrow mountain roadways for slower-moving vehicles (p. 312)
...da de incorporación carril derecho adicional en las carreteras de montaña estrechas destinado a los vehículos de marcha más lenta

ramp meter a set of traffic signals—red and green only—used to control traffic flow onto a highway (p. 327)
semáforos de ramal de enlace un conjunto de semáforos (sólo de luz roja y verde) utilizados para controlar la circulación del tránsito que entra en una autopista

reaction distance distance your vehicle travels while you react (p. 174)
distancia de reacción distancia que recorre el vehículo mientras reacciones

señal reglamentaria señal que controla el tránsito

reversible lane a lane in which traffic can travel in either direction, depending on conditions, often used during commuter hours (p. 330)
carril reversible carril en el cual el tránsito puede desplazarse en una u otra dirección, dependiendo de ciertas condiciones, utilizado frecuentemente durante las horas pico

ride the brake resting your foot on the brake pedal while driving (p. 282)
montar el freno conducir con el pie puesto sobre el pedal del freno

right of way privilege of having immediate use of a certain part of a roadway (p. 189)
derecho de paso privilegio de usar inmediatamente cierta parte de una carretera

right-turn-on-red turning right when the red signal is on, permitted at most intersections (p. 28)
giro a la derecha en rojo girar a la derecha cuando el semáforo está en rojo, permitido en la mayoría de las intersecciones

risk in driving, the possibility of having a conflict that results in a collision (p. 4)
riesgo al conducir, la posibilidad de tener un conflicto que produzca una colisión

risk factor anything that can increase the possibility of a collision (p. 80)

1.1 You Are Part of the System

Words and Ideas

risk: *Risk* means danger. The main risk in driving is the possibility of colliding with something or someone.

highway transportation system (HTS): This is made up of people, vehicles, and roadways.

roadway users: The people who use the HTS by walking, driving, or riding are called roadway users.

Name ______________________________ Date ______________

chapter 1
Companion

vehicle: Anything you can drive or ride to go from one place to another is a vehicle. Bicycles, cars, sport utility vehicles, buses, motorcycles, and trucks are all vehicles.

regulate: To regulate means to control or direct according to a rule or law.

driver's license: *License* means permission by law. A driver's license means you have permission to drive. Your state will give you permission to drive (a driver's license) when you have learned the driving laws and have passed the driving tests.

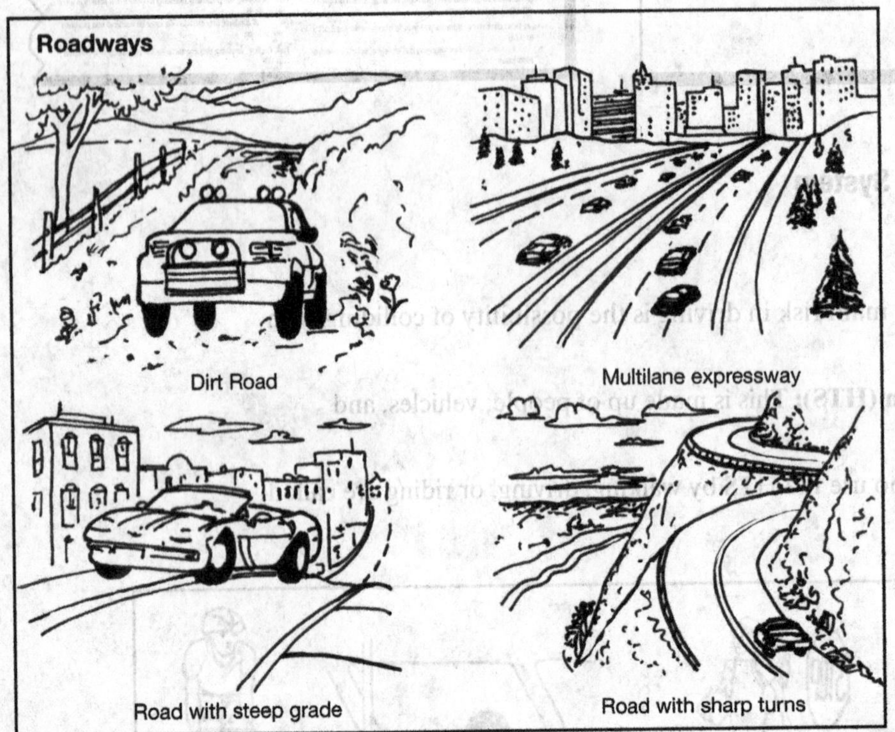

Think About It

1. On which roadway may you drive faster? ______________________________

2. On which roadway must you drive more slowly and carefully?

____

Name ______________________ Date ____________

1.2 Your Driving Task

Words and Ideas

driving task: The driving task requires social, physical, and mental skills.

skills: Skills are learned abilities that require practice and experience to become good. Your skill as a driver will get better as you practice driving.

courteous driver: A courteous driver is polite to others and makes an extra effort to think about other drivers.

The IPDE Process

IPDE stands for **Identify, Predict, Decide,** and **Execute.** Each word will help you with driving by helping you see, think, and act in all situations. Remember these four steps in the IPDE Process and use them every time you drive.

I = Identify: To *identify* means to look for and find something. When you drive, look for and identify important information, such as road signs and signals, other vehicles on the road, and possible problems.

P = Predict: To *predict* means to think about and guess. Use all your experience, knowledge, and judgment to predict what will happen next. When driving you must be able to predict what other drivers will do.

D = Decide: To *decide* means to choose what to do. When you drive you must decide quickly how to act and when to act.

E = Execute: To *execute* means to act or to do something. When driving you must execute actions that keeps you and others safe.

The IPDE Process

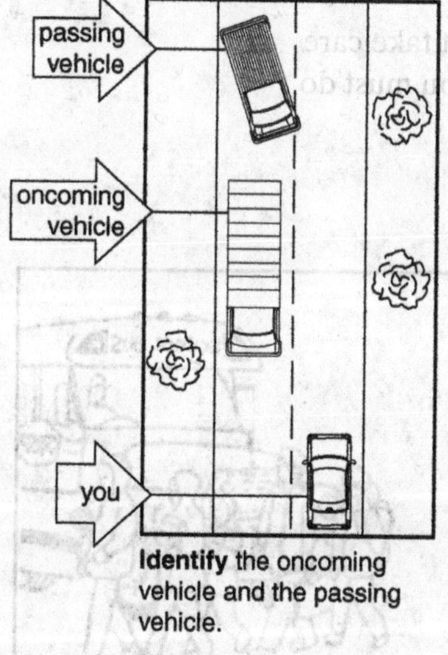

Identify the oncoming vehicle and the passing vehicle.

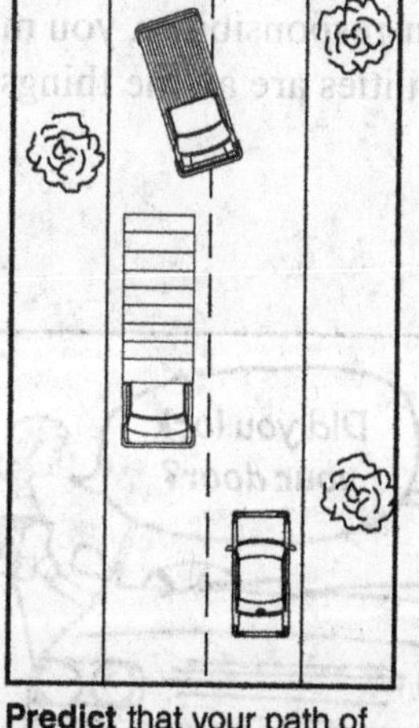

Predict that your path of travel and the passing vehicle's path of travel will collide.

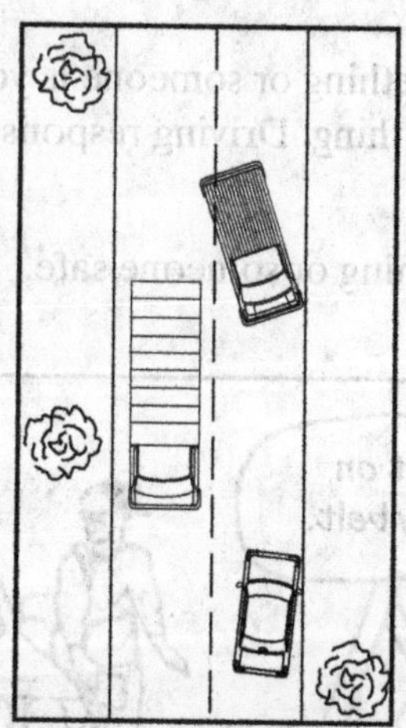

Decide to slow and move to the side of the road.

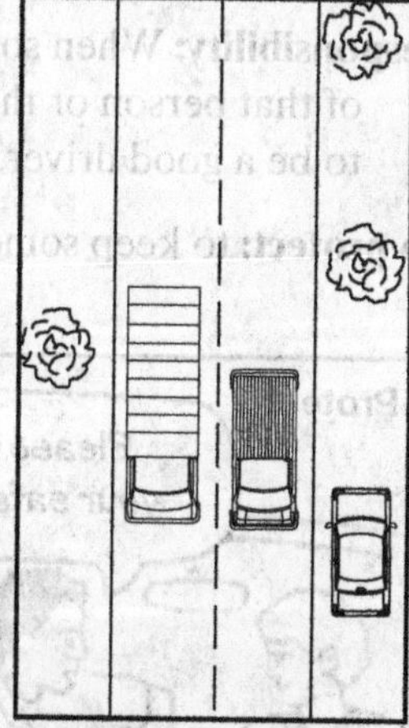

Execute your decision by driving to the side of the road and letting the truck pass.

Zone Control System: This is a method for managing the space around your vehicle.

low-risk driving: Low-risk driving is a driving method in which you keep track of other vehicles and people around you, and do not assume that they will act the way you think they should. This reduces the risk of a collision.

1.3 Your Driving Responsibilities

Words and Ideas

operating costs: These are costs that depend on how much driving you do, or how much you operate the vehicle. These costs include fuel, oil, and tires.

fixed costs: These are costs that do not depend on how much driving you do. These include the cost of the vehicle itself, the costs of a driver's license, and insurance costs.

collision: A collision is when there is contact between two or more objects, as when two vehicles collide—crash—into each other.

responsibility: When something or someone is your responsibility, you must take care of that person or that thing. Driving responsibilities are all the things you must do to be a good driver.

to protect: to keep something or someone safe.

Protect your passengers. Protect your property. Protect other roadway users.

Name ______________________________ Date ______________

efficient: If something is efficient, it works well and does not waste energy.

fuel-efficient: A fuel-efficient vehicle does not waste fuel. A fuel-efficient car goes more miles on one gallon of gasoline than a car that is non-fuel-efficient.

fuel consumption: Fuel consumption means to use fuel.

Think About It

Read the following statements, then circle the best answer—**a** or **b.**

1. A friend offers you a beer while driving. Should you
   a. say no and ask him or her to not drink in your car.
   b. have a drink so your friend won't feel offended.
2. Two cars were going fast on a wet road. They collided with each other. The police officer's report said they were in
   a. an accident.
   b. a collision.
3. In adverse weather conditions, you should
   a. drive the way you usually do and get home as fast as possible.
   b. slow down.
4. A fuel-efficient car is good to have because
   a. it costs less to buy.
   b. our air stays cleaner because we use less fuel.

Name ______________________________ Date ______________

1.4 Your Driver's License

Words and Ideas

graduated driver licensing program: This program requires young drivers to go through different stages to get a driver's license. The program helps reduce collisions.

learner's permit stage: Young drivers receive a permit to drive with supervision for 6 to 12 months.

intermediate license stage: The learning driver has certain limits on driving and may have more hours of supervision for 6 to 18 months. There may be limits on night driving and the age and number of passengers.

full-privilege license stage: Once you have completed the intermediate license stage without a traffic ticket or collision, you will receive a driver's license without limits.

Think About It

Write *True* or *False* for each statement in the space provided.

1. You must always wear a safety belt when driving. ______________

2. You must never drink and drive. ______________

3. You do not need to practice driving to become a good driver. ______________

Name ______________________ Date ____________

Learning New Words

Take a look at Chapter 2 to familiarize yourself with the topics covered. Look for all the highlighted words in **dark** print. These are the vocabulary words. Write the words on a sheet of paper, then write the meaning next to each word.

2.1 Traffic Signs

Words and Ideas

regulatory sign: To *regulate* means to control. Regulatory signs tell drivers what to do. They control traffic and tell you about laws that you must obey.

warning sign: To *warn* means to let people know about dangers. Warning signs help you avoid surprise situations and tell you that danger is ahead.

guide sign: Guide signs show you where to go. They help find routes, intersections, service areas, and other points of interest or information. Guide signs tell you how to get places.

yield: You allow the other car to go before you when you yield.

right of way: You can use the roadway first when you have the right of way.

intersection: An intersection is where two roads meet each other.

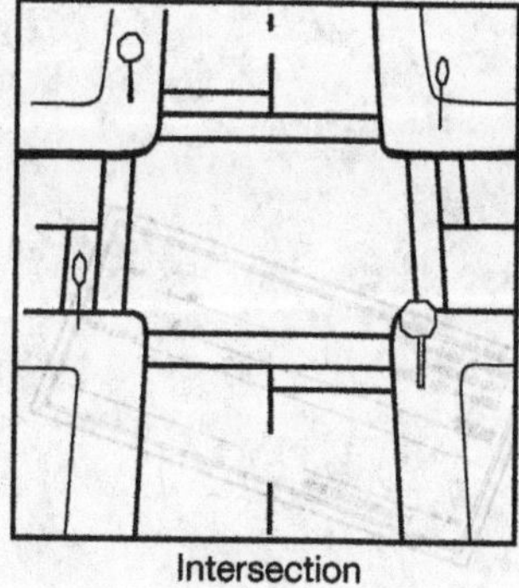
Intersection

Name ______________________________ Date ______________

STOP sign: STOP signs are used on a road that crosses a main highway or a through street. A full stop is required.

proceed: To proceed means to go forward.

oncoming traffic: Oncoming traffic is traffic that is coming toward you.

crosswalk: A crosswalk is an area marked with white lines where pedestrians cross a street. Cars must stop at crosswalks and let pedestrians cross the street.

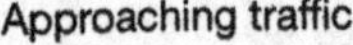
Approaching traffic

Pedestrian in the crosswalk

Double Trouble

Some words have two or more meanings. Study the meanings for each word.

full: **(1)** opposite of empty; filled up. *Example:* I can't eat any more. I'm full. **(2)** complete; total; 100%. *Example:* When Karina approached the STOP sign, she came to a full stop.

check: **(1)** to look around and see, to look for something. **(2)** a special piece of paper you use instead of money. **(3)** a mark ✔

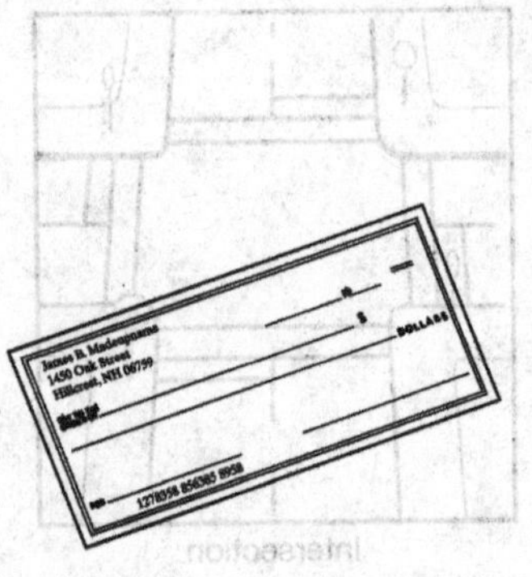

Name ______________________ Date __________

speed limit signs: Speed limit signs tell you how fast you may drive when driving conditions are ideal.

ideal: Ideal means the best. Ideal weather conditions are as follows: The sun is shining. You can see very far. There is no rain or snow. The roads are not wet or slippery.

basic speed law: When conditions are not ideal, the basic speed law says you must drive at a speed that is safe for existing conditions.

maximum: Maximum means the most, the highest. Maximum speed limit means the fastest you are allowed to drive, under ideal conditions.

minimum: Minimum means the least, the lowest. Minimum speed limit means the slowest you are allowed to drive, under ideal conditions.

advisory speed limits: These are speed limits set for special conditions, such as sharp curves.

Speed limit sign

Think About It

Fill in the blanks with one of the following:

- basic speed law
- minimum speed limit
- advisory speed limit

1. When driving under dangerous weather conditions, you want to observe the ______________________.
2. When driving on an expressway, you'll want to pay attention to the maximum speed limit and the ______________, which is set to keep traffic moving safely.
3. When approaching a curve, look for the ______________ which may be posted below a warning sign.

school zone: This is a portion of a road near a school that is subject to special speed limits.

crossing guard: This person gives directions in a school zone. You must obey the crossing guard and stop when asked.

construction zone: A construction zone, or work zone, is an area where something is being built or the road is being repaired.

Name ______________________________ Date ______________

chapter 2
Companion

railroad crossing: where a road crosses railroad tracks

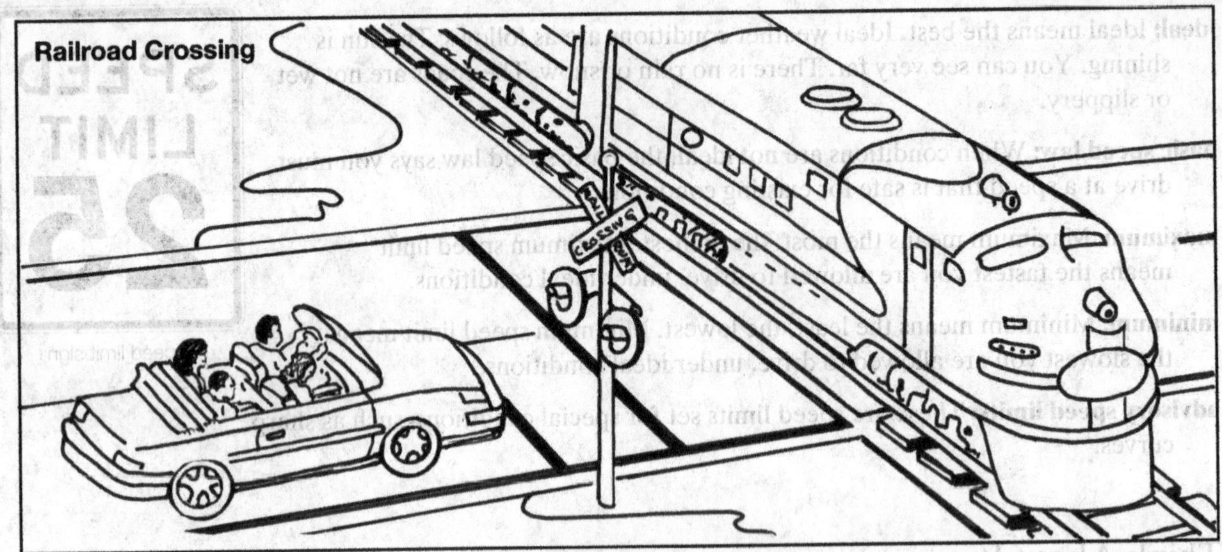

Never cross a railroad track when the red lights are flashing or the gates are down.

route: Road. The route marker tells you the number of the road. Local, state, U.S., and interstate routes are posted with route signs. Even numbers are east-west routes. Odd numbers are north-south routes.

international symbols: symbols used on traffic signs that give a message without using words

Road Narrows

Think About It

Look at the signs below. Write the correct name of the sign on the line provided. Choose from the following list:

- railroad advance-warning sign
- school zone sign
- construction sign
- no passing sign
- school crossing sign

1. ______________

2. ______________

3. ______________

4. ______________

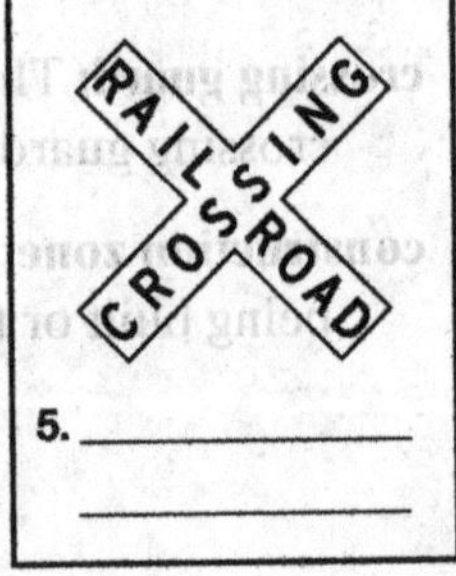

5. ______________

Name ______________________________ Date ____________

Think About It

Circle the best answer.

1. When you approach a school zone, you should
   a. look for children, then slow down.
   b. slow down and look for children.
   c. speed up to get through the school zone faster.

2. The maximum speed is
   a. the speed you must always drive.
   b. the highest speed you may drive under ideal conditions.
   c. the slowest speed you can drive.

3. At every STOP sign you must
   a. come to a full stop before proceeding.
   b. slow down.
   c. stop and count to 50 before going ahead.

2.2 Traffic Signals

Words and Ideas

traffic signal: Traffic signals are colored lights or signs that tell drivers or pedestrians what to do.

flashing signal: A flashing signal is a light that goes on and off. It warns you to slow down or stop.

Figure It Out: Find the Picture

Below is a list of different traffic signals. Find a picture of each in *Drive Right*, pages 27–30. Write the page number next to the correct traffic signal.

1. traffic light ______________ 3. flashing light ______________
2. arrow ______________ 4. pedestrian signal ______________

directional arrows: Directional arrows point the direction that traffic must flow. They are also used to tell you when you can turn at an intersection.

pedestrian signal: This signal tells pedestrians whether they should walk or wait to cross the street.

rush hour: Rush hour is during the time of day when many people are going to and from work. There is a morning rush hour and an evening rush hour in and around most cities.

lane signal: This is a signal, usually overhead, that tells whether a lane can or cannot be used at a specific time.

right-turn-on-red: You can turn right when the red signal is on unless there is a sign that says you may not.

Go straight ahead when arrow is green

traffic control officer: This person tells cars when and where to go. The officer uses hand signals to direct traffic.

2.3 Roadway Markings

Words and Ideas

roadway markings: Lines, arrows, or words are painted on the road to give you a warning or direction.

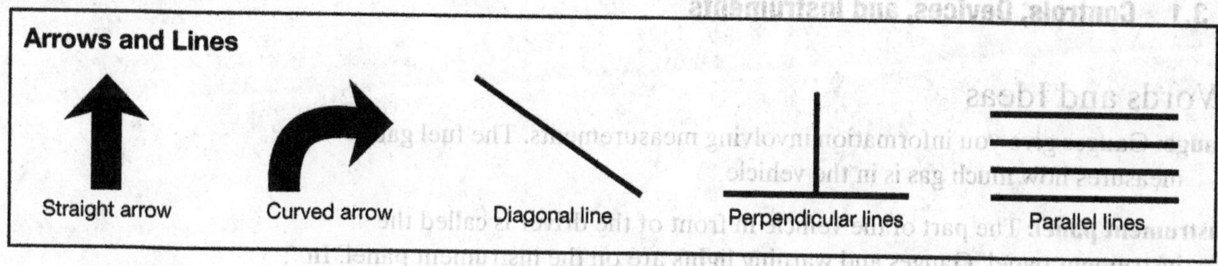

Roadway arrows give directions.

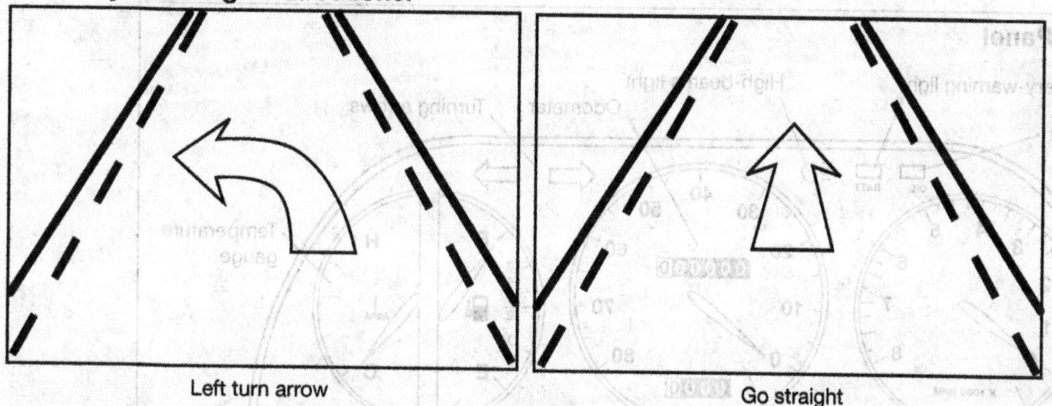

shared left-turn lane: This is a lane on a busy street that helps drivers make safer left turns in the middle of a block.

rumble strips: These are short sections of bumpy roadway that warn you that you are approaching a dangerous area. They are also used to warn that you are driving too close to the edge of the road.

reflective markers: Raised or lowered roadway markers are small reflectors along the road to help you see the driving lane in the dark.

color coded: Different colors are used to show different meanings. White roadway markers show the edge of a road. Red roadway markers warn that you are driving in the wrong direction.

fire hydrants: A fire hydrant provides water when there is a fire.

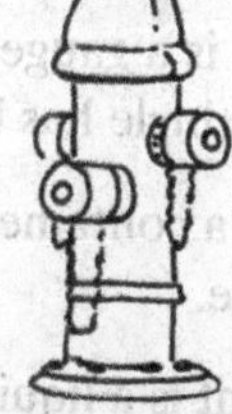
Fire hydrant

Handicapped parking

reserved: When parking spaces are reserved they are saved for use by certain people.

handicapped parking: Some parking spaces are reserved for people with special physical needs.

Name ______________________ Date ______________

chapter 3
Companion

Learning New Words

Take a look at Chapter 3 to familiarize yourself with the topics covered. Look for all the highlighted words in **dark** print. These are the vocabulary words. Write each word on a sheet of paper, then write the meaning next to each word.

3.1 Controls, Devices, and Instruments

Words and Ideas

gauge: Gauges give you information involving measurements. The fuel gauge measures how much gas is in the vehicle.

instrument panel: The part of the vehicle in front of the driver is called the instrument panel. Gauges and warning lights are on the instrument panel. In different models of vehicles, the gauges may be in different places.

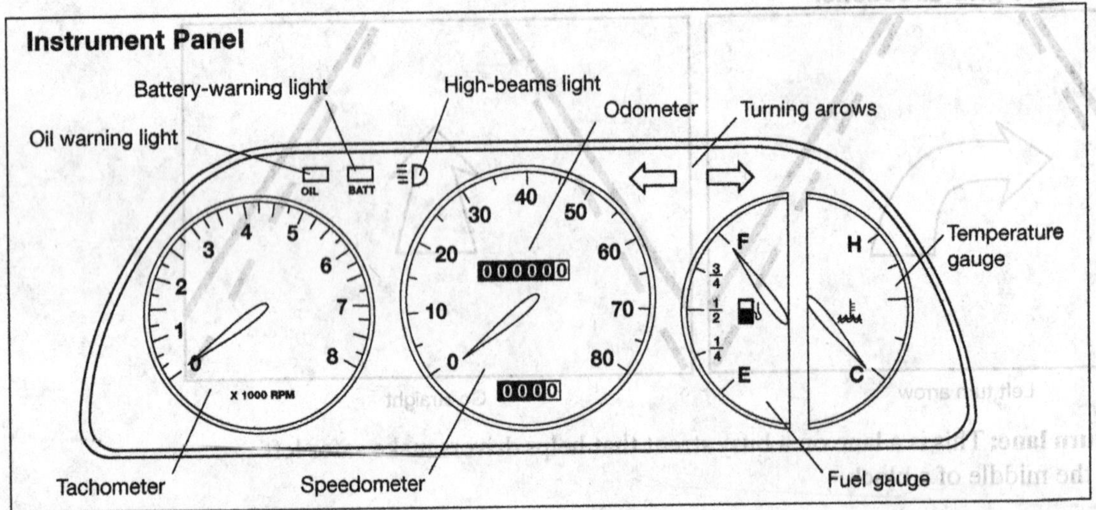

indicator lights: The lights on your vehicle's instrument panel indicate—show you—something about the vehicle. A safety belt light is an indicator that warns you that you have not fastened your safety belt.

odometer: This is a gauge on the instrument panel that indicates the total number of miles the vehicle has been driven.

tank: A tank is a container that holds liquids. The fuel tank holds the gasoline for your vehicle.

coolant: Coolant is a liquid that helps keep the engine cool.

circulate: To circulate means to move through or around. Oil must circulate through the vehicle's engine.

pressure: Pressure is force or strength. To protect the engine, the oil must circulate at the right pressure. The oil gauge on the vehicle's instrument panel indicates the oil pressure.

Name ______________________ Date __________

alternator warning light: This is a light or gauge on the instrument panel that warns you that the battery is being drained.

generate: To generate is to make. The alternator generates electricity to run the vehicle.

battery: A car battery is a part that stores (holds) electricity used by the vehicle.

drained: A battery that is being drained is losing electricity.

Think About It

Look at the fuel gauge on the right, then answer the following questions in the space provided.

1. What does the F stand for? ______________________

2. What does the E stand for? ______________________

3. Does the fuel gauge show almost full or almost empty? ______________

4. The gas tank in your vehicle holds 12 gallons. It is now 3/4 full. How many gallons do you have left? ______________________

5. The gas tank in your vehicle holds 12 gallons of gas. If you get 30 miles per gallon, how many miles can you drive on a full tank?

____

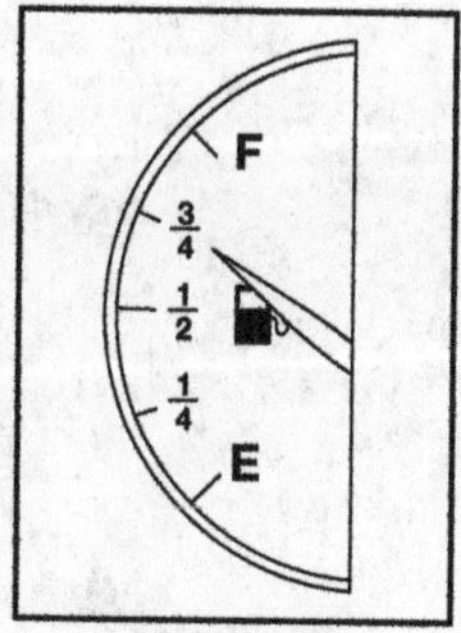

Fuel gauge

Name ______________________ Date __________

antilock braking system: This braking system keeps the wheels from locking if the driver brakes hard.

air bag: An air bag is a safety device found in newer vehicles. It is located in the steering wheel of the driver's side and above the glove compartment on the passenger's side. It is a balloon that inflates on impact.

brake lights: These are white lights at the rear of your vehicle that tell others that you are backing.

high-beam headlights: These are the strongest and brightest lights on the vehicle. You need high-beam headlights when you are driving in very dark conditions and there are no other vehicles on the road. Switch to low-beam headlights (regular headlights) when you see oncoming traffic.

shift indicator: This is the device on the vehicle that shows the different driving gears and the one being used.

lever: A lever is a bar or handle that you use to make changes. A shift lever changes gears.

Levers

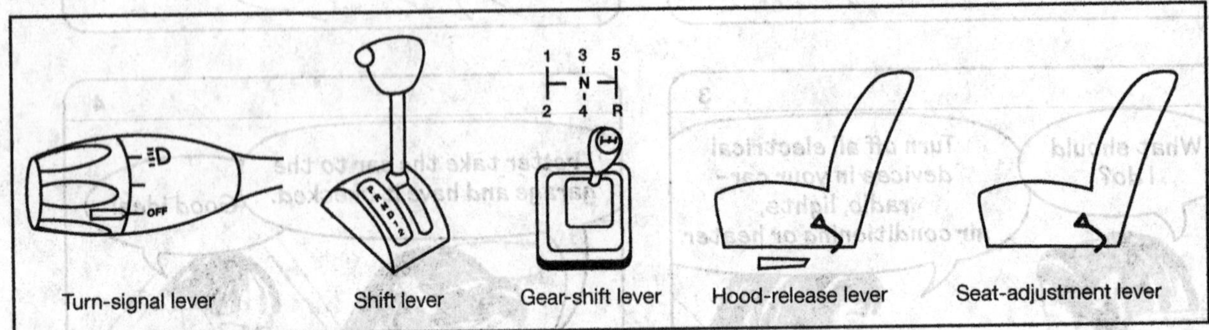

cruise: To cruise is to move at a steady speed.

cruise control: This is a device that lets you maintain your desired speed without keeping your foot on the accelerator.

release: To release means to let go. Before you can drive, you must release the parking brake.

Name ____________________ Date ____________

Automatic Transmission Gears

P

PARK: This gear locks the transmission.

R

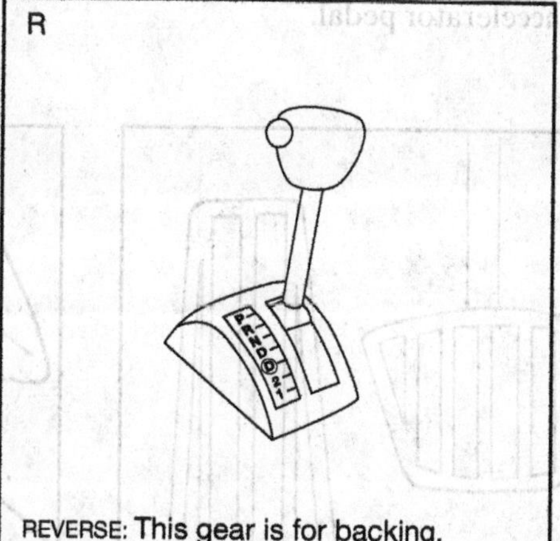

REVERSE: This gear is for backing.

N

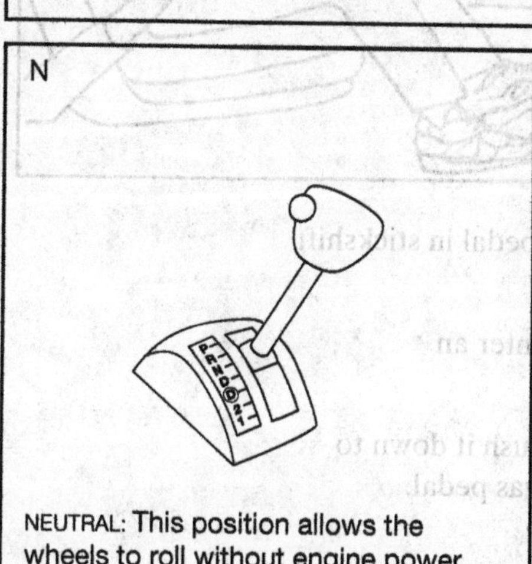

NEUTRAL: This position allows the wheels to roll without engine power.

D

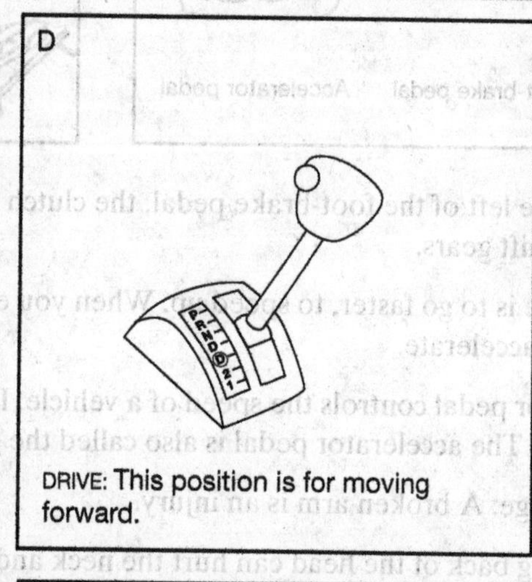

DRIVE: This position is for moving forward.

Ⓓ

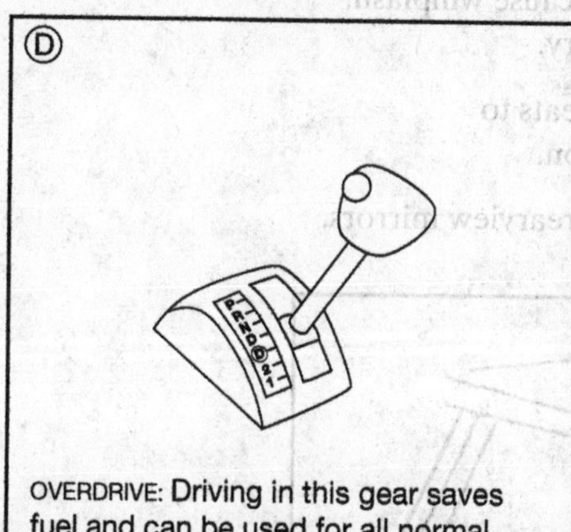

OVERDRIVE: Driving in this gear saves fuel and can be used for all normal driving over 40–45 mph.

L1

L1 and L2 or 1 and 2: These positions allow the engine to send more power to the wheels at lower speeds. Both are for slow, hard pulling and for going up and down steep hills.

pedal: A pedal is a lever that you operate with your foot, such as a clutch pedal, foot-brake pedal, and accelerator pedal.

Pedals

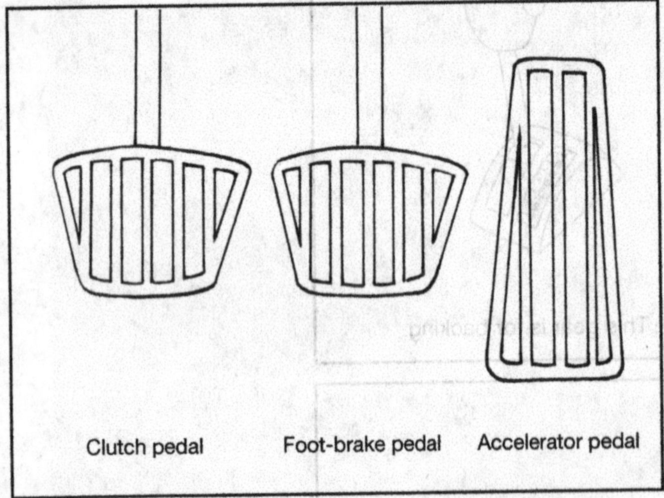

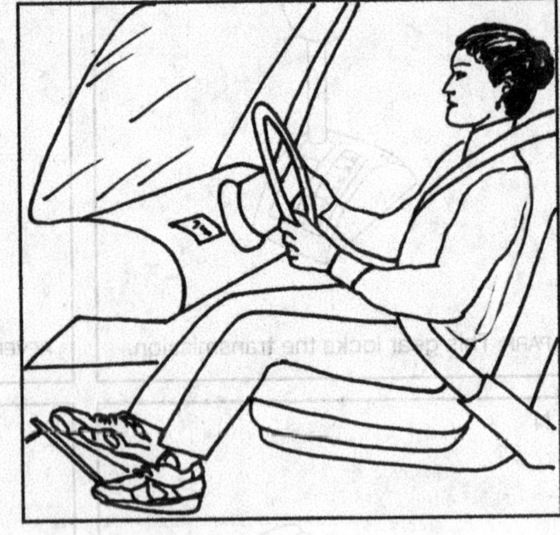

clutch pedal: Located to the left of the foot-brake pedal, the clutch pedal in stickshift vehicles lets a driver shift gears.

to accelerate: To accelerate is to go faster, to speed up. When you enter an expressway, you must accelerate.

accelerator: The accelerator pedal controls the speed of a vehicle. Push it down to make the car go faster. The accelerator pedal is also called the gas pedal.

injury, injuries: hurt, damage. A broken arm is an injury.

whiplash: A sudden moving back of the head can hurt the neck and cause whiplash. In a collision, the driver and passengers may get a whiplash injury.

head restraints: These padded devices are on the back of the front seats to help reduce whiplash injuries—injuries to the neck—in a collision.

blind-spot areas: These are areas that you are not able to see in the rearview mirrors.

Vehicle Mirrors

Name ______________________________ Date ______________

3.2 Getting Ready to Drive

Words and Ideas

procedure: A procedure is a set of steps to follow.

inspect: Before you begin to drive, you'll want to inspect—look over—the vehicle.

oil marks: A wet, dark spot under the vehicle could be an oil stain. Always have a mechanic check if you have any doubt.

adjust: To adjust is to move something to make it fit better. Adjust the vehicle seat so that you can reach the pedals and feel comfortable.

3.3 Starting, Stopping, Steering, and Targeting

Words and Ideas

ignition switch: Operated by a key, this switch starts or stops the engine.

accessory: This is a position on the starter switch that can be used to run accessories, such as lights, radios, or CD players, without running the engine.

controlled steering: When you use controlled steering, you are taking an active role in making sure you have a comfortable grip on the steering wheel to help reduce injury and keep control during collisions.

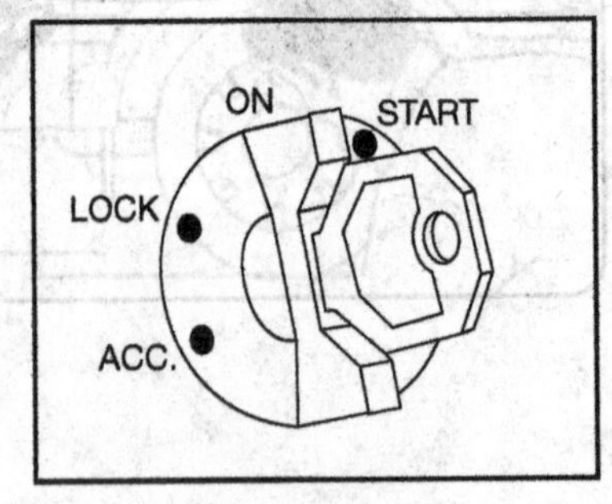

Ignition switch

target: A target is what you are aiming for when you drive. Look for a fixed object that appears in the distance in the center of the path you intend to drive.

fixed: A fixed object is one that does not move.

hand-over-hand steering: This is pulling the steering wheel down with one hand while the other hand crosses over to pull the wheel farther down.

hand-to-hand steering: This is pushing the steering wheel up with one hand and pulling it down with the other hand.

3.4 Driving a Vehicle with Manual Transmission

Words and Ideas

transmission: This is the part of a vehicle that turns engine speed into power to turn the wheels.

manual transmission: A vehicle with a manual transmission has a clutch and a gear-shift control that you use to shift gears. The gears do not shift automatically.

clutch: This is a pedal that helps you shift gears in a manual transmission vehicle.

semi-automatic transmission: A vehicle with a semi-automatic transmission has no clutch. The driver can shift gears manually simply by moving the shift lever.

Double Trouble

Each of the words below has more than one meaning. One meaning is given to you. You can find the other meaning in the Words and Ideas sections of this chapter. Write the other meanings you find next to each word below.

a. transmission: (1) a radio or television signal

(2) ______________________________

b. clutch: (1) to grab or hold on to

(2) ______________________________

Name ______________________ Date ____________

Learning New Words

Take a look at Chapter 4 to familiarize yourself with the topics covered. Look for all the highlighted words in **dark** print. These are the vocabulary words. Write the word on a sheet of paper, then write the meaning next to each word.

4.1 Mirror Usage and Backing Procedure

Words and Ideas

backing: Backing is a maneuver in which you drive your vehicle backward.

convex: When a mirror is convex, it has a rounded surface like the curve of a ball.

crawl: To crawl is to move slowly.

obstruction: An obstruction is an object that blocks your intended path of travel.

straight: A straight path is one without bends or curves.

Figure It Out: Steering Backward

Look at these pictures as you read the section on steering backward in *Drive Right* on page 65. Then under each picture, write the correct instructions. The first one is done for you.

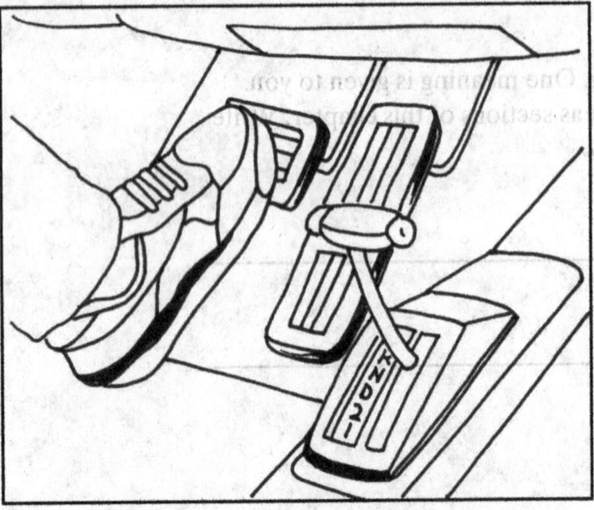

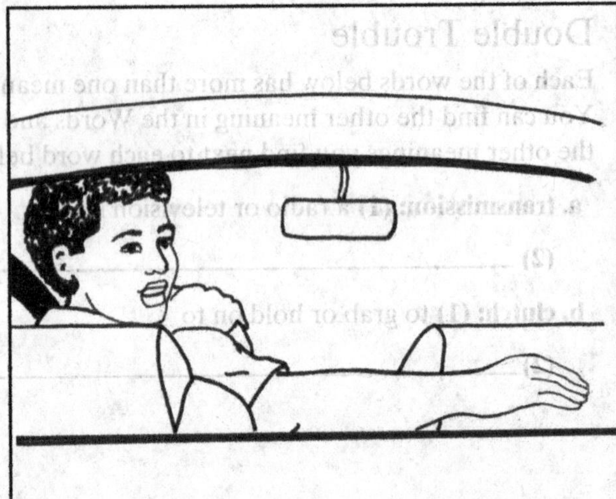

1. Hold the brake pedal down and shift to REVERSE.

2. ______________________

Name ______________________ Date __________

chapter 4
Companion

3. ______________________

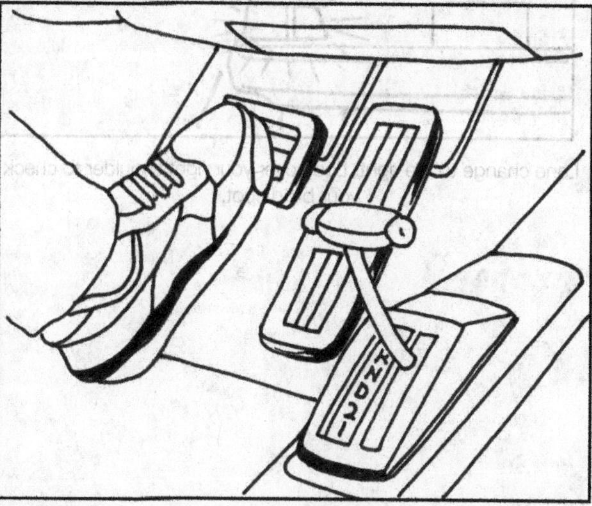

4. ______________________

Think About It

Why do you keep your foot over the brake pedal while the vehicle moves backward?

____

Name ______________________ Date ____________

4.2 Basic Driving Maneuvers

Words and Ideas

lane changes: When you change lanes, you move from one lane to another.

hand signals: Use your left arm for hand signals. Use your right hand to maintain steering. Use hand signals when your turn-signal lights do not work or in bright sunlight when your turn-signal lights may be hard for other drivers to see.

Changing Lanes: Blind-Spot Check

Lane change to the left: Look over your left shoulder to check your blind spot.

Lane change to the right: Look over your right shoulder to check your blind spot.

midblock: *Mid-* means in the middle or halfway. Midblock is in the middle of the block.

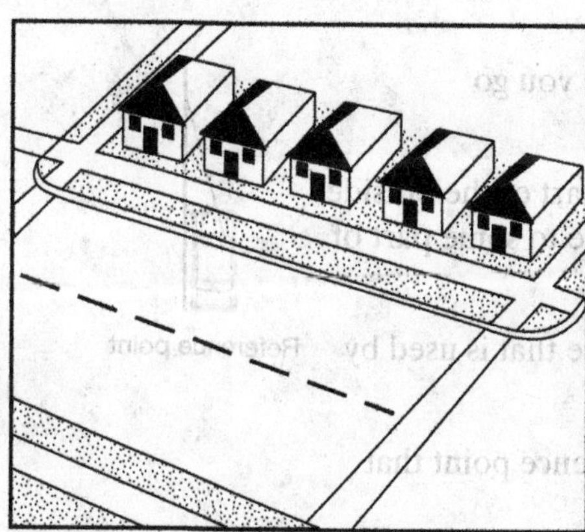
A block of houses

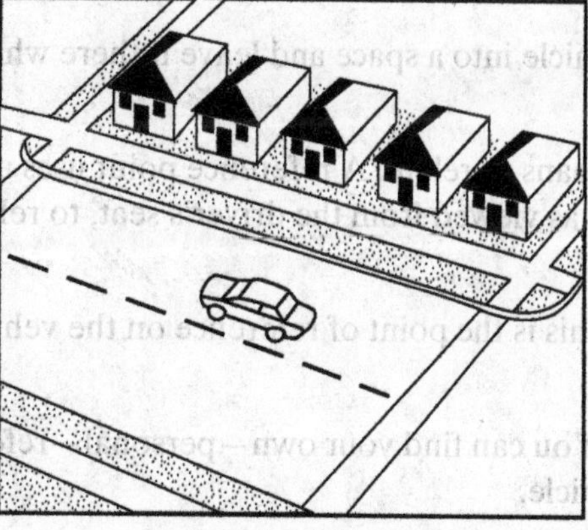
A car in midblock

turnabout: A turnabout is a maneuver for turning your vehicle around to go in the opposite direction.

maneuver: A maneuver is a specific, planned movement.

U-turn: A U-turn is a turnabout maneuver where you turn around on the roadway and go in the opposite direction.

re-enter: To re-enter is to enter again. When you turnabout in a driveway, you can then re-enter traffic.

avoid: Avoid means to stay away from. Avoid turnabout maneuvers that put you at risk.

Name ______________________ Date ____________

4.3 Parking Maneuvers

Words and Ideas

park: To park is to put a vehicle into a space and leave it there while you go elsewhere.

reference point: To refer means to relate. A reference point uses a part of the outside or inside of the vehicle, as viewed from the driver's seat, to relate to some part of the roadway.

Reference point

standard reference point: This is the point of reference on the vehicle that is used by most drivers.

personal reference points: You can find your own—personal—reference point that works for your own vehicle.

angle parking: This is parking the vehicle diagonally to the curb.

diagonally: To park diagonally is to park in places that are on a slant or angle.

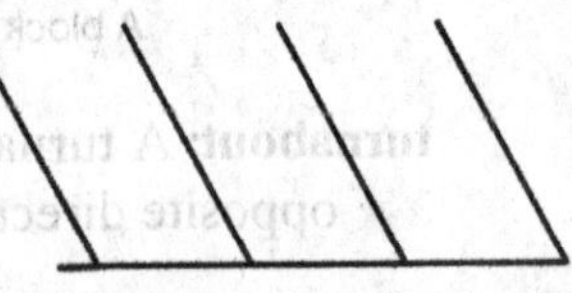

Angle parking

straighten: To straighten means to make straight. To straighten the tires of your vehicle, turn the steering wheel.

Wheels turned to right

Wheels straightened

perpendicular parking: This is when you park your vehicle at a right angle to the curb.

right angle: A right angle is an angle of 90°.

Right angle

bumper: This is a bar across the front and back of a vehicle. Bumpers protect a vehicle from damage when it is bumped—hit.

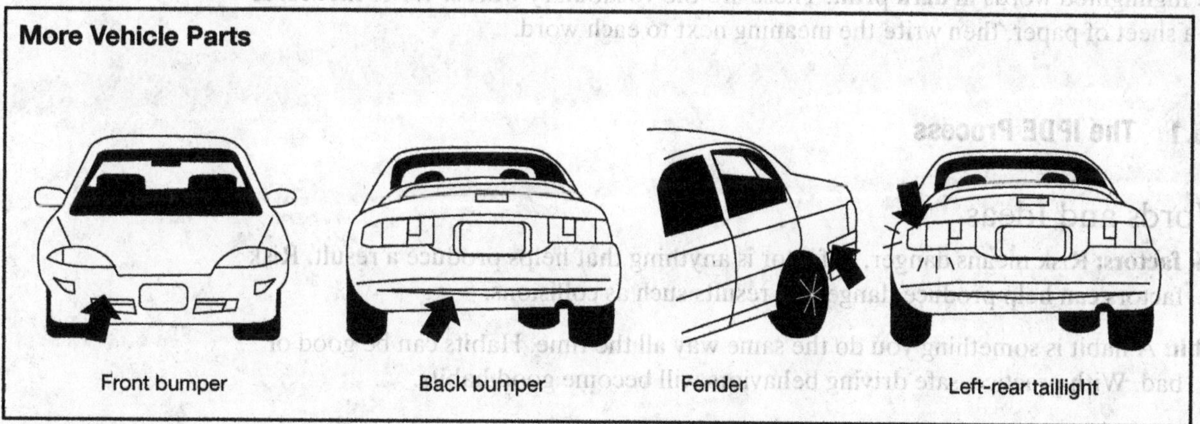

parallel parking: This is when you park your vehicle parallel to the curb.

parallel: When your vehicle is parallel to the curb, both the front and back of the vehicle are the same distance from the curb.

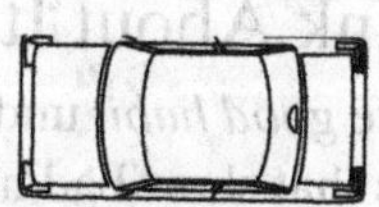
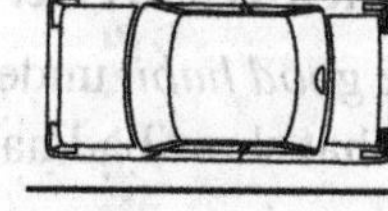
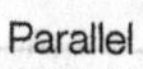

Think About It

Circle the letters of the correct answer or answers.

1. For parallel parking, you need to
- **a.** back into a parking space.
- **b.** use your turn signals.
- **c.** use your horn.

2. Learning to park is
- **a.** a necessary part of learning to drive.
- **b.** a good idea but isn't necessary to learn.
- **c.** only necessary for getting your driver's license.

3. When you drive straight backward, you need to
- **a.** look in your rearview mirror only.
- **b.** look back through the rear window.
- **c.** keep your foot over the brake pedal.

Name ______________________________ Date ____________

chapter 5
Companion

Learning New Words

Take a look at Chapter 5 to familiarize yourself with the topics covered. Look for all the highlighted words in **dark** print. These are the vocabulary words. Write the words on a sheet of paper, then write the meaning next to each word.

5.1 The IPDE Process

Words and Ideas

risk factors: Risk means danger. A factor is anything that helps produce a result. Risk factors can help produce dangerous results such as collisions.

habit: A habit is something you do the same way all the time. Habits can be good or bad. With practice, safe driving behaviors will become good habits.

Think About It: Habits

Write *good habit* under the pictures that show good habits. Write *bad habit* under the ones that show bad habits.

1. ____________ **2.** ____________ **3.** ____________ **4.** ____________

ability: Your ability is what you are able to do.

analyze: To analyze something is to look at all the parts. When in heavy traffic, you should analyze the situation to decide what to do.

critical clues: Critical clues are extremely important pieces of information that you must pay attention to.

identify: The first step in the IPDE Process is to identify—to look for and find—possible hazards.

reading traffic situations: When you are driving, you see and analyze important clues. When you read traffic situations, you are able to predict what will happen.

hazards: Hazards are dangers that you will encounter as a driver, such as icy roads.

predict: The second step in the IPDE Process is to predict—to make a guess—about what could happen. You will use your knowledge, judgment, and experience.

conflict: Conflict is a problem situation. In driving, a conflict is when you and another driver get in the way of each other. As a driver, you will need to identify and predict possible conflicts and take action to assure your safety.

Name ______________________________ Date ____________

chapter 5
Companion

Think About It: The IPDE Process

In the boxes, write a description of each step in the IPDE Process.

1. Identify Hazards	2. Predict Conflict

3. Decide	4. Execute

Name ______________________ Date ______________

chapter 5
Companion

5.2 Identify and Predict

Words and Ideas

Zone Control System: This system helps you control the space—six zones—around your vehicle. It allows you to see and respond to changes in the zones so that you can control the traffic situation.

zone: A zone is an area of space that is the width of a lane and extends as far as the driver can see. There are six zones around a vehicle.

open zone: This is the space where you can drive safely in your intended path of travel.

line of sight: This is the distance you can see ahead in the direction you are looking. If your line of sight is restricted, that zone is closed.

restriction: To restrict means to not allow. If something does not allow you to see ahead, such as a truck, your line of sight is restricted.

path of travel: This is the space your vehicle will occupy as you travel ahead.

target area: Your target is the aiming point where you want to go. The target area is the section of the roadway where the target is located and the area to its right and left.

closed zone: This is a space not open to you to travel safely. A zone can be closed by a restriction in your line of sight, another vehicle, or a traffic light or sign.

Think About It

Look at the drawing below that shows closed zones. Choose from the following list the phrase that corresponds to the correct number in the picture.
Write the phrase in the space provided.

- closed front zone
- closed rear zone
- closed front-right zone

1. ______________________
2. ______________________
3. ______________________

Closed Zones

Name ______________________ Date ____________

orderly: Orderly means organized, following a plan.

visual: Visual means using the eyes, seeing.

orderly visual search pattern: This is a planned way of looking for clues about driving situations.

Orderly Visual Search Pattern

1. Look ahead to target area.

2. Evaluate the left-front, front, and right-front zones in the 12–15-second range.

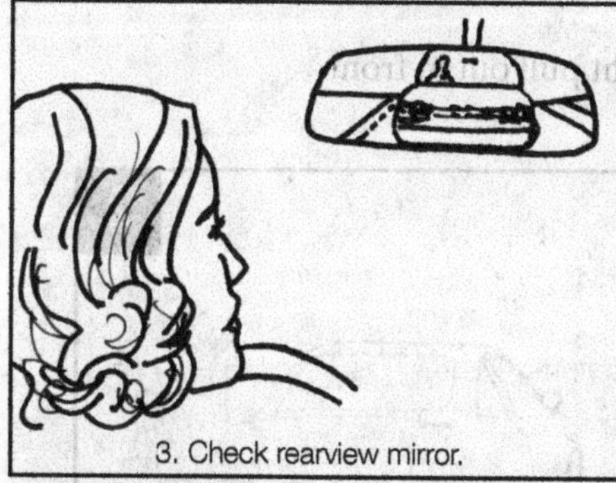
3. Check rearview mirror.

4. Evaluate your 4–6-second range.

5. Look ahead.

6. Check your 4–6-second range.

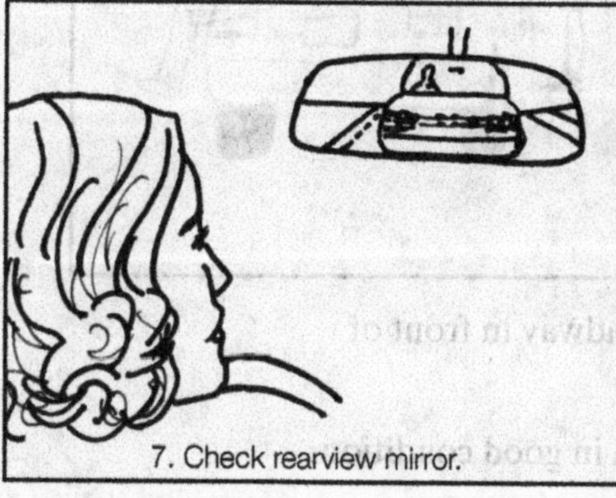
7. Check rearview mirror.

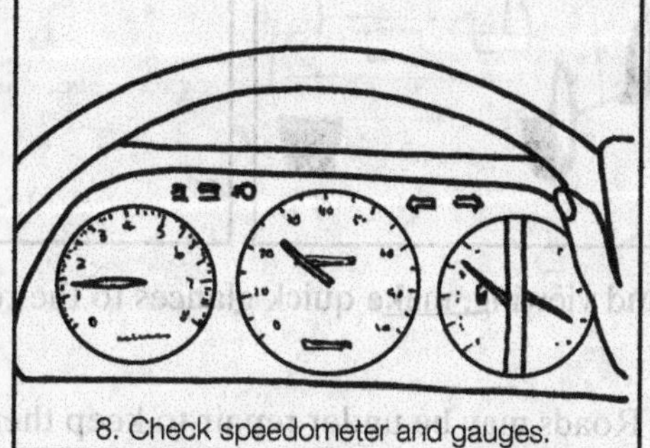
8. Check speedometer and gauges.

Name ______________________________ Date ______________

searching ranges: A searching range is a distance ahead of you where you are to search as you drive. You search to evaluate your intended path of travel.

field of vision: The area you can see around you while looking straight ahead is called your field of vision.

central vision: This is the center part of your vision in which you can see clearly while looking straight ahead.

peripheral vision: This is your side vision to the left and right of your central vision. You see less clearly to the side of your central vision.

fixate: To fixate on something is to stare at it for a long time.

scanning: Scanning is looking at all parts of a large area quickly.

selective seeing: Selective means to choose only what is important. Selective seeing means you identify and choose only those clues and events that restrict your line of sight or can change your intended path of travel.

Think About It: Driving Detective

Which of the following situations have clues that tell you a car might pull out in front of you?

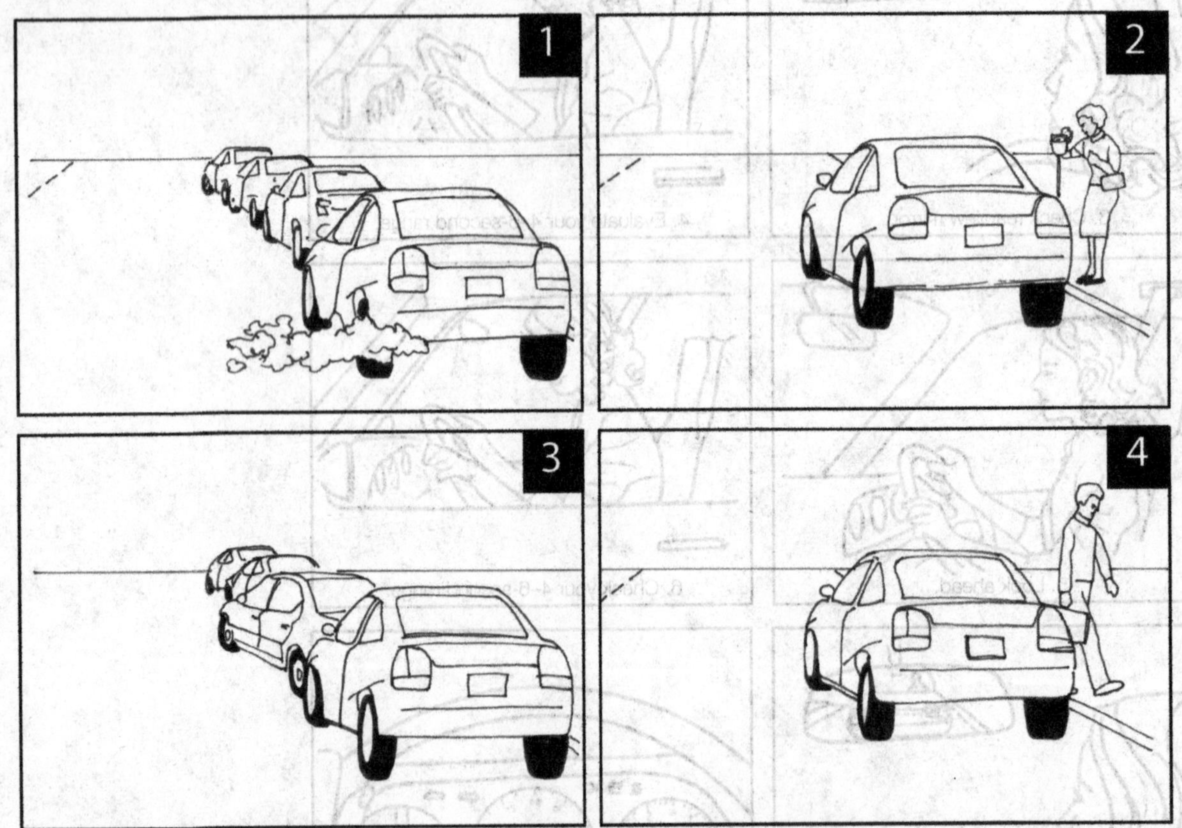

ground viewing: For ground viewing, make quick glances to the roadway in front of your vehicle.

repair: To repair is to fix. Roads may be under repair to keep them in good condition. Watch for construction areas where roads are being repaired.

through lane: The portion of road that is open for driving ahead is the through lane.

gravel: small pieces of rock

roadway surface: The top layer of the road is the surface. It may become slippery when wet.

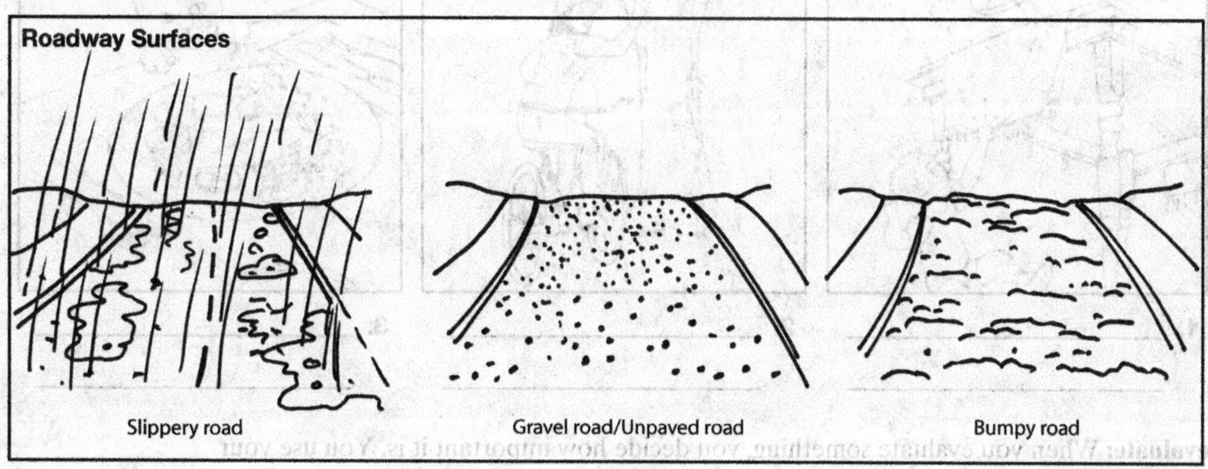

sliding: When you are sliding, you are moving across a smooth surface.

skidding: When you are skidding, you are sliding without any control. A vehicle may skid on a slippery road.

traffic controls: Traffic lights, STOP and YIELD signs, and flashing lights are all examples of traffic controls. Traffic controls are designed to control the flow of traffic.

overhead: Overhead is above your head. Traffic lights may be overhead.

Figure It Out: Hazards

Identify three possible hazards in the picture below. On a separate sheet of paper, write a sentence about each hazard. *Example:* The bicyclist might come into my lane to avoid the car pulling out of the driveway.

Name ______________________ Date ____________

chapter 5
Companion

Think About It: Predictions

Write a prediction for each picture below.

1. ______________________
____

2. ______________________
____

3. ______________________
____

evaluate: When you evaluate something, you decide how important it is. You use your knowledge, information, and feelings to evaluate.

safe-driving memory bank: The more you drive and the more knowledge you gain from the study of traffic laws and driver-education materials, the more you add to your safe-driving memory bank. This bank will help you identify and predict more quickly and accurately and increase your chances of becoming a low-risk driver.

judgment: To judge means to think about something and make a decision. Making a judgment about a traffic situation involves measuring, comparing, and evaluating.

experience: The more you drive, the more experiences you have. Experience gives you a solid base for making sound judgments.

speed: Speed—how fast you drive—is the most important factor in maintaining control of your vehicle.

traction: Traction is the ability of the tires to grip the roadway surface.

Name ______________________ Date ____________

5.3 Decide and Execute

Words and Ideas

decide: The third step in the IPDE Process is to decide, or choose. You decide on the best action to take, when to take the action, how to take the action, and where to go with the action in order to avoid possible conflicts.

execute: The fourth step in the IPDE Process is to execute—to carry out—your decision. You may change your speed, steer, or communicate.

decelerate: When you take your foot off the accelerator pedal, the vehicle will decelerate, or slow down.

accelerate: When you push down on the accelerator pedal, the vehicle will accelerate, or speed up.

steer: When you steer a vehicle with the steering wheel, you are guiding the direction the vehicle will go.

space cushion: This is an open area around a vehicle.

Ways to Communicate to Other Drivers

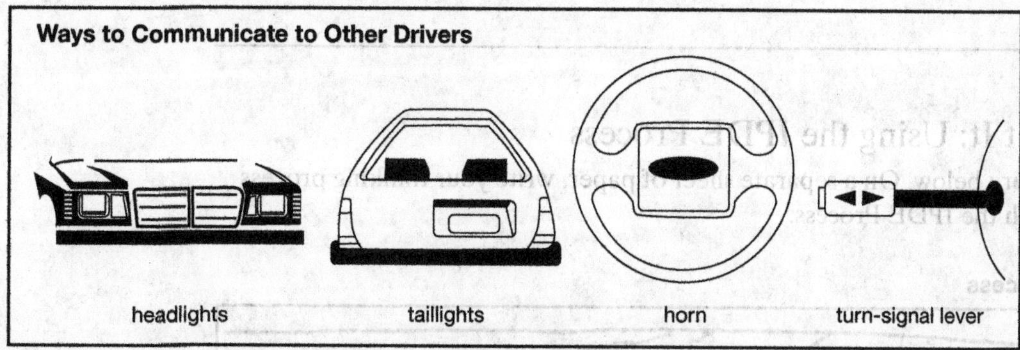

minimize a hazard: To minimize is to make less. To minimize a hazard is to lessen the chance of a dangerous situation or a conflict.

separate the hazards: This is the process of adjusting the speed of a vehicle to handle one hazard at a time when two or more hazards threaten a driver.

compromise space: Reduce your risk by giving as much space as possible to the greater of two or more hazards.

disabled: When a vehicle is disabled, it is not running properly. Disabled vehicles along the roadway are a hazard. If your vehicle is disabled, pull to the side of the road and turn on the hazard flasher lights.

combine actions: When you drive you will execute more than one action at a time. You will be combining actions, such as accelerating and steering at the same time.

5.4 Using the IPDE Process

Words and Ideas

selective: To be selective is to pick and choose. When using the IPDE Process selectively, you may choose to begin a new cycle before completing all four steps.

Think About It

Write *True* or *False* for each statement.

1. In every driving situation, you will need to use all four steps of the IPDE Process.

____

2. When someone else is driving, you can practice the I, P, and D steps of the IPDE Process.

____

3. When you become an experienced driver you don't need to use the IPDE Process anymore.

____

Think About It: Using the IPDE Process

Look at the picture below. On a separate sheet of paper, write your thinking process as you go through the IPDE Process.

Use the IPDE Process

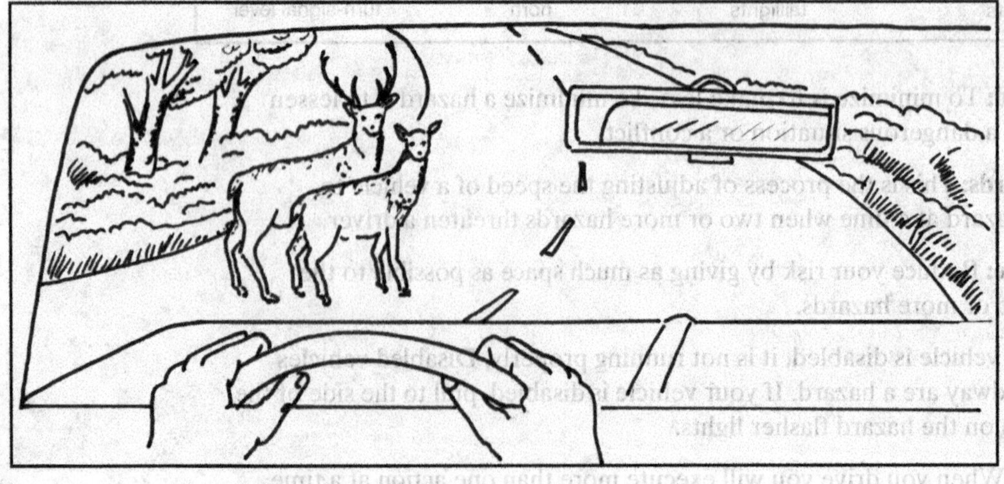

Name ____________________ Date ____________

Learning New Words

Take a look at Chapter 6 to familiarize yourself with the topics covered. Look for all the highlighted words in **dark** print. These are the vocabulary words. Write each word on a sheet of paper, then write the meaning next to the word.

6.1 Emotions and Driving

Words and Ideas

emotion: An emotion is a strong feeling, such as anger, fear, or joy.

assess: To assess is to evaluate, to judge. When you assess a driving situation, you decide whether there is any danger ahead.

revenge: Revenge means to get even. Driving is no place to seek revenge.

stressful: If something is stressful, it is upsetting and makes you feel nervous.

fatigue: Fatigue means to be tired. Stressful driving can cause fatigue.

assumptions or expectations: Assumptions or expectations are things you think are true. You have certain assumptions or expectations about the drivers around you. Your assumptions or expectations may not be true.

react: To react to something is how you act when something happens.

aggressive: To be aggressive is to act in a forceful or hostile way. A driver may react aggressively to another driver's action by showing anger, tailgating, or honking and flashing lights.

rage: Rage is great anger. It is anger that is out of control.

sorrow: Sorrow is a feeling of sadness.

depression: Depression is a state of unhappiness.

anxiety: Anxiety is a feeling of worry and nervousness.

irresponsible: The opposite of responsible, to make irresponsible errors is to make careless or reckless errors.

peer pressure: Your peers are people in your age group. Peer pressure is the pressure you feel from your peers to do something.

distract: This means to take your attention away. When a passenger distracts the driver, it can be dangerous.

refrain: To refrain is to avoid or not take part. To refrain from heated discussions is to avoid them.

reckless: To be reckless is to be careless, to do dangerous or harmful things. Reckless actions put you and your passengers in danger.

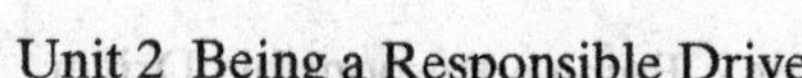

intervene: To intervene is to come between or to interfere. When a driver is acting reckless and you intervene, you encourage the driver to let someone else drive.

endanger: To endanger is to put at risk. Do not endanger your safety or the safety of others.

potential: This is something that could happen. Always be aware of potential dangers when driving.

habits: A habit is something we do over and over until we hardly even realize we are doing it.

gestures: Gestures are motions you make with your hands or other parts of your body to indicate something to someone.

Think About It: Feelings and Emotions

Below each picture write the word or words that best describe the emotion. Choose from the following list of words.

anger   excitement   heated discussion   depression

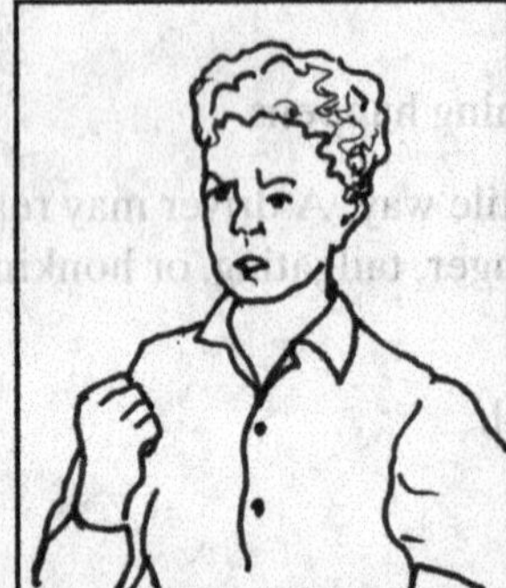

1. ______________ 2. ______________ 3. ______________

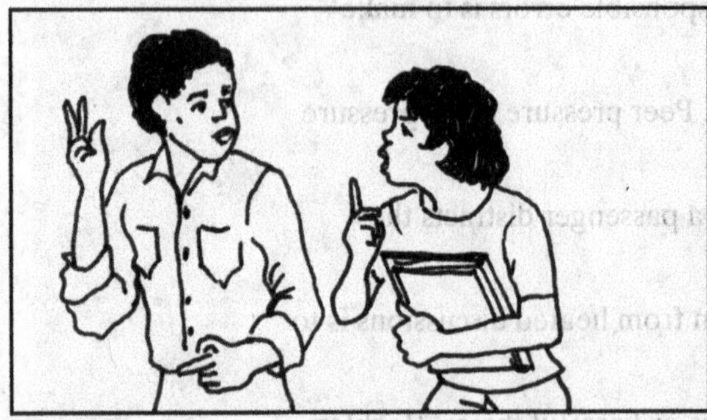

4. ______________________________

Name ______________________ Date ____________

6.2 Physical Senses and Driving

Words and Ideas

visual acuity: This is your ability to see things clearly both near and far away.

field of vision: Your field of vision is everything you can see when you are looking straight ahead.

tunnel vision: This is a narrow field of vision of 140° or less. Someone with tunnel vision cannot see well to the sides.

fringe vision: This is the part of your peripheral vision that is closest to your central vision.

color blindness: This is not being able to see any difference between some colors.

depth perception: This is the ability to judge distance between yourself and other objects.

night blindness: This is not being able to see well at night.

glare: Glare is very bright light that makes it difficult to see well. Glare occurs when bright sunlight or headlights are reflected off shiny surfaces.

glare resistance: This is the ability to continue seeing when looking at bright lights.

glare recovery time: This is the time your eyes need to be able to see clearly after being affected by glare.

Name ______________________________ Date ______________

chapter 6
Companion

Think About It

Read the following questions, then answer them in the space provided.

1. Why is it harder to see at night? ______________________________

____

2. List three things you can do that can protect your eyes from glare.

____

____

____

speed smear: This occurs when objects off to your sides appear blurred and unclear as your speed increases.

6.3 Physical Disabilities

Words and Ideas

disability: Somebody with a disability has trouble doing a certain thing, or cannot do it at all. One example of a disability is blindness. A blind person cannot see. Disabilities can be temporary, which means they last only for a little while, or permanent, which means they cannot be changed.

physical: Something physical has to do with the body, not the mind. Not being able to walk is a physical disability.

side effect: Side effects are the unwanted things that a medicine can do to you. A medicine that helps your headache might have a side effect of upsetting your stomach. Many cold medicines may make you drowsy.

carbon monoxide: This is a colorless, odorless, tasteless gas that is in your vehicle's exhaust fumes.

odorless: Odorless means without any smell. You cannot smell an odorless gas.

fumes: Fumes are gas, smoke, or vapor.

nausea: You have nausea when you have a sick feeling in your stomach.

combat: To combat is to fight. To combat the effects of carbon monoxide exposure is to take actions to lessen its effect on you.

traffic jams: Traffic jams happen when traffic is so heavy that it comes to a stop.

smoke residue: A yellow film from smoking covers your vehicle's windows and makes it more difficult to see.

compensate: To compensate is to make allowances for. When you take medicine and drive, you must compensate for side effects by using extra caution.

chronic illness: A chronic illness is a sickness that lasts for years.

Name ________________________________ Date ______________

Learning New Words

Take a look at Chapter 7 to familiarize yourself with the topics covered. Look for all the highlighted words in **dark** print. These are the vocabulary words. Write each word on a sheet of paper, then write the meaning next to the word.

7.1 Effects of Alcohol on Driving Safely

Words and Ideas

fatally injured: A fatally injured driver is a driver who dies as a result of a collision.

abuse: Abuse is to use something on purpose in a wrong, harmful, or illegal way. Teens often abuse alcohol by drinking and driving.

underage: Underage means younger than the legal age for doing something. All states have laws that say you must be 21 years old to drink alcohol. If you are younger than 21, you are underage for drinking alcohol.

vigorously enforced: Laws that are vigorously enforced are laws that are strictly kept. If you are underage and caught drinking, you will be punished.

rate: This is the number measured in proportion to (in comparison with) something else. Drivers under age 21 are involved in fatal crashes because of drinking at twice the rate of drivers aged 21 and older.

impaired: Someone who is impaired by alcohol is someone whose abilities are weakened by alcohol.

abstain: To abstain means to not do something. To abstain from drinking alcohol means to not drink.

central nervous system: Your central nervous system is your brain, spinal cord, and nerves. This is the part of your body that controls how you act, move, and behave.

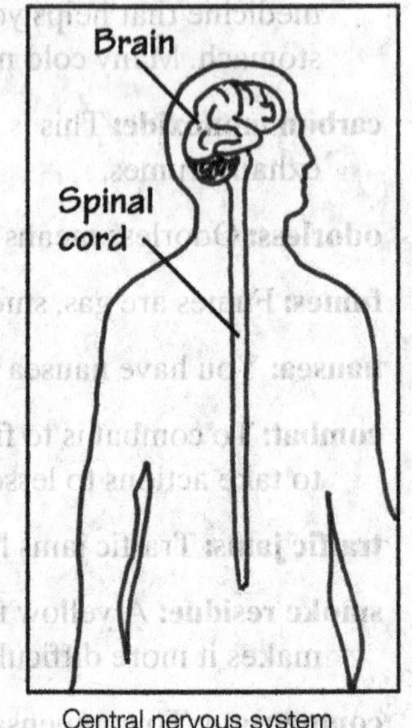

Central nervous system

anesthetic: Anesthetics cause total or partial loss of sensations from the nerves for touch and other senses; they lessen your ability to function normally.

mental skills: These are your thinking and reasoning skills.

physical abilities: These are the abilities and actions of your body.

euphoria: This is a false sense of well-being developed as a result of use of alcohol or drugs.

erratic: This means lacking consistency; wandering.

distort: To distort is to twist out of a normal pattern. Alcohol distorts vision so that a person does not see clearly.

fixate: When your eyes fixate on something, they stare at it for a long time.

inhibitions: Inhibitions are inner forces of personality that restrain or hold back one's impulsive behavior.

reflex: A reflex is something your body does automatically. One's eye reflex—the ability of eyes to adjust from darkness to light and from light to darkness—is impaired by alcohol.

excessive: This means too much. Excessive drinking is too much drinking, drinking until one's abilities are impaired.

alcoholism: This is a disease in which a person cannot stop drinking and is addicted to alcohol.

blood alcohol concentration (BAC): This is the amount of alcohol in the blood. When a person drinks alcohol, the alcohol gets into the blood and is measured by the percent of alcohol in the bloodstream. For legal purposes, a person with a BAC of 0.08 percent or more is considered intoxicated (drunk) and unable to drive safely. However, a smaller BAC can make a person unsafe to drive.

intoxication: Intoxication is having too much alcohol in your bloodstream to drive. Someone who is intoxicated is drunk.

proof: This describes the strength of alcohol (beer, wine, or liquor). The higher the proof, the stronger the alcohol.

absorption rate: This is the rate at which alcohol is absorbed in—how fast it is taken into—your body.

oxidized: When something is oxidized, it is mixed with oxygen. When the alcohol in your system is oxidized, it is mixed with the oxygen in your body and then removed by the liver.

designated driver: This is the person who is chosen to drive everyone home from a party or other group event. The designated driver does NOT drink.

Figure It Out: Fatal Crashes

Look over the charts on pages 132 and 133 of *Drive Right*, then circle the right answer.

1. If you have one beer, how many hours do you need to wait before driving?
- **a.** 5 to 7 hours
- **b.** 1/2 hour
- **c.** 1 1/2 hours

2. If you have 2 glasses of wine, how many hours do you need to wait before driving?
- **a.** 3 hours
- **b.** 4 to 5 hours
- **c.** 1 3/4 hours

Name ______________________________ Date ______________

chapter 7
Companion

7.2 Other Drugs and Driving

Words and Ideas

over-the-counter (OTC) medicine: This is a drug you can buy at the store without a prescription.

prescription: a written note from a doctor for medicine

pharmacist: A pharmacist is a person trained in drugs and medicines. Your pharmacist can tell you about the effects of different medicines.

prescription medicine: These are drugs that can be bought legally only when ordered by a doctor.

depressant: This drug can slow down the central nervous system. Depressants are used to treat nervousness and high blood pressure. Alcohol is a depressant.

stimulant: A stimulant is a drug that speeds up the central nervous system.

amphetamines: These drugs are a type of stimulant.

hallucinogens: These are illegal drugs that can cause a false sense of things.

marijuana: This is an illegal drug that causes distortion in one's mental and physical abilities.

antihistamine: This is an over-the-counter medicine that is taken for colds and allergies. Antihistamines can cause drowsiness or have other side effects that may impair your ability to drive.

synergistic effect: Mixing of two or more substances can multiply the effects of both. This is called a synergistic effect.

Think About It

Write *True* or *False* for each statement.

1. Over-the-counter drugs can't impair (harm or weaken) your driving skills. ________

2. Alcohol is not a drug. ________

3. If you are not driving, it is OK to mix alcohol and other drugs. ________

Name ______________________________ Date ____________

7.3 Traffic Laws Governing the Use of Alcohol

Words and Ideas

consume: To consume is to eat or drink; to take into your body.

consent: This means to agree.

implied consent law: Every state has this law which states that anyone who gets a driver's license automatically agrees to be tested for blood-alcohol content and other drugs if stopped for suspicion of drug use while driving.

illegal *per se* laws: *"Per se"* means "by itself" in Latin. An illegal *per se* law is a law making it illegal to drive after drinking alcohol or using drugs, even if no other laws are broken.

driving while intoxicated (DWI), driving under the influence (DUI), operating while impaired (OWI): These are different ways of naming the law against driving if you have a blood alcohol concentration that is more than 0.08 percent. Every state has this law, but different states use different names for it.

zero tolerance law: Most states have zero tolerance laws that say it is illegal for persons under the age of 21 to drive with any measurable amount of alcohol in the blood.

intoxilyzer: This is a machine that tests a person's breath for blood-alcohol content.

field sobriety test: These are on-the-spot, roadside tests that help an officer detect whether a driver is sober or under the influence of alcohol or other drugs.

nystagmus: This is an involuntary jerking of the eyes as a person gazes to the side. One type of field sobriety test determines when nystagmus begins.

penalty, penalties: This is punishment. Penalties for DUI and DWI may include suspension of your driver's license, fines, or prison terms.

conviction: When you have been proven guilty of DUI or DWI, there has been a conviction.

suspension: This means to take away for a certain period of time, or suspend. Suspension of your driver's license is a punishment for an offense such as DUI or DWI.

revocation: This means to cancel, or to revoke. Revocation of your driver's license means the loss of your driver's license as punishment for an offense, such as conviction of a DUI or DWI.

fine: A fine is the amount of money paid as a penalty for breaking the law.

prison term: This is the amount of time someone stays in a prison or jail as punishment for breaking the law.

manslaughter: This is the killing of another person without meaning to hurt anyone.

murder: This is the killing of another person with the intent to hurt someone.

What to Do If a Police Officer Stops You
• Slow down. • Pull to the right and stop in a safe place. • Have your driver's license ready to show the officer. • Stay in your car and wait for the officer to tell you what to do. • Keep your hands where the officer can see them. • Be polite, and answer the officer's questions honestly.

7.4 Coping with Peer Pressure

Words and Ideas

peer pressure: This is the influence that people of a similar age have over you and how you behave.

peer education: This is an organized program in which young people help other young people make decisions and determine goals.

peer influence: This is the desire to be accepted.

Ways to Say No

1. Be firm.

2. Prepare reasons.

3. Suggest alternatives.

4. Walk away.

Learning New Words

Take a look at Chapter 8 to familiarize yourself with the topics covered. Look for all the highlighted words in **dark** print. These are the vocabulary words. Write the words on a sheet of paper, then write the meaning next to each word.

8.1 Driver Inattention and Distraction

Words and Ideas

driver inattention: This is when the driver stops paying attention to the driving task.

fatigue: Fatigue means extreme tiredness.

distracted driving: This is when something in particular takes the driver's attention away from the driving task.

distraction: A distraction is something that takes attention from something else.

visual: Visual means having to do with sight or seeing. When a distraction is visual, it takes your eyes away from the road.

cognitive: A cognitive distraction takes your mind off the task of driving. Cognitive means the act, process, or power of thinking.

biomechanical: When a distraction is biomechanical, you are using your body to do something other than driving. Biomechanical means having to do with the movement or function of the body.

auditory: Auditory means having to do with the sense of hearing.

Types of Distractions

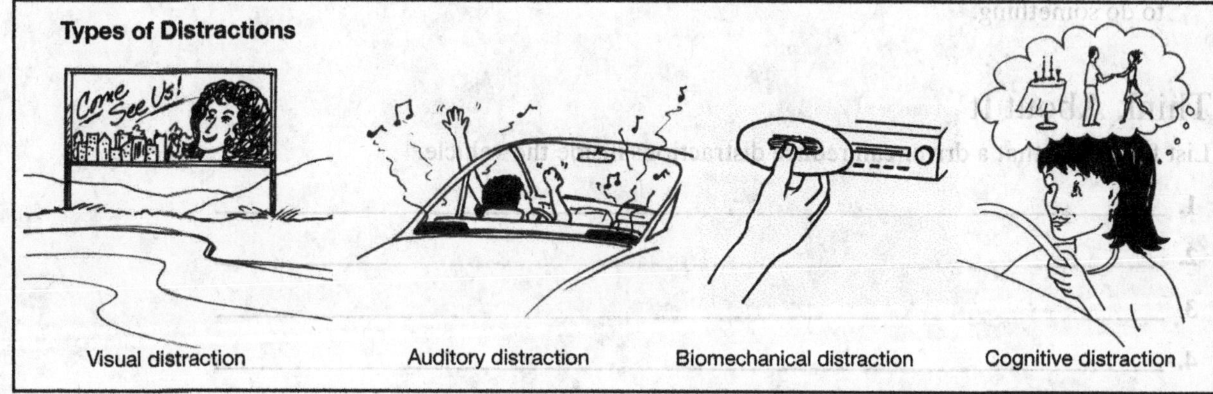

Visual distraction | Auditory distraction | Biomechanical distraction | Cognitive distraction

Name ______________________________ Date ______________

8.2 Distractions Inside the Vehicle

Words and Ideas

luxury: A luxury item is one that few people are able to afford.

substantial: A substantial number of people means many people.

opportunities: Opportunities are chances for something to happen.

projectile: This is an object that is thrown by an outside force.

multimedia: This means having several forms of communication. Many new phones have multimedia systems that allow the user to take pictures, play music, watch videos, and browse the Internet.

navigational: A navigational system helps you find your way around an unfamiliar place.

capabilities: A device's capabilities are the things that it can do.

hands-free technology: This term refers to devices that allow a person to use a cell phone without using his or her hands. A headset is one type of hands-free technology.

ordinance: An ordinance is a law.

allergic: Someone who is allergic to a substance becomes sick when they are exposed to it.

extreme: An extreme case is one that is very much out of the ordinary.

disruptive: If people are being disruptive, they are interrupting a person who is trying to do something.

Think About It

List four ways that a driver can reduce distractions inside the vehicle.

1. ______________________________

2. ______________________________

3. ______________________________

4. ______________________________

Name ______________________ Date ____________

8.3 Distractions Outside the Vehicle

Words and Ideas

commitment: Commitment means dedicating yourself to accomplishing something.

potential: Potential is the possibility for a situation to turn out a certain way.

informative: Something that is informative gives you valuable information.

gawking: This is another word for staring.

rubbernecking: This is when a person continually looks all around the scene of a collision.

backlog: When there is a traffic backlog, the cars are traveling at a slow pace and create a line that extends down the roadway.

perimeter: A perimeter is a boundary enclosing a specific area.

Think About It

Explain how gawking and rubbernecking can cause more harm than just distracting other drivers.

____

____

____

____

Think About It

Write *True* or *False* for each statement.

1. Inside-the-vehicle distractions are easier to deal with than outside-the-vehicle distractions.

   ____

2. If you are driving and you see an interesting animal that you want to look at, you should find a safe place to pull over and stop your vehicle.

   ____

3. Short messages on electronic traffic signs help keep the signs from distracting drivers.

   ____

4. It is not dangerous to take your eyes off the road as long as you are doing it to look for emergency vehicles.

   ____

5. When exiting a crowded parking lot after a sporting event, it is important to pay attention to crowds and their actions as well as the traffic around you.

   ____

Learning New Words

Take a look at Chapter 9 to familiarize yourself with the topics covered. Look for all the highlighted words in **dark** print. These are the vocabulary words. Write the words on a sheet of paper, then write the meaning next to each word.

9.1 Gravity and Energy of Motion

Words and Ideas

natural laws: A natural law explains why things happen in nature. The law of gravity is a natural law. The law of gravity explains why apples fall down, not up, from a tree.

gravity: The force of gravity pulls all things to Earth.

energy of motion: This is energy an object has because it is moving.

control: To control your vehicle is to handle it safely.

force: Force is strength or power.

inertia: resistance to a change in motion or at rest

momentum: the habit of an object to stay in motion

Name ______________________ Date ____________

Energy of Motion

Name ______________________________ Date ______________

double: To double is to multiply by two. To double the number 9, multiply by 2; that is, $9 \times 2 = 18$. A box weighs 9 pounds. Double the weight of the box is 18 pounds. If you are driving 20 miles an hour, double your speed is 40 miles an hour.

four times: Four times means to multiply by 4. Four times 9 would be 36; that is, $9 \times 4 = 36$. If you are driving 20 mph, four times your speed is 80 mph.

square of a number: The square of a number is the number you get when you multiply a number by itself. The square of 2 is 4; that is, $2^2 = 2 \times 2 = 4$. The square of 3 is 9; that is, $3^2 = 3 \times 3 = 9$.

Think About It: Energy of Motion

Look at the pictures below, then circle the correct answer for each question.

Car A is going 35 miles per hour.

Car B is going 40 miles per hour.

1. Which car has more energy of motion?
   a. car A **b.** car B
2. Which car will need more time and distance to stop?
   a. car A **b.** car B
3. Which car is obeying the speed limit?
   a. car A **b.** car B

9.2 Tires and Traction

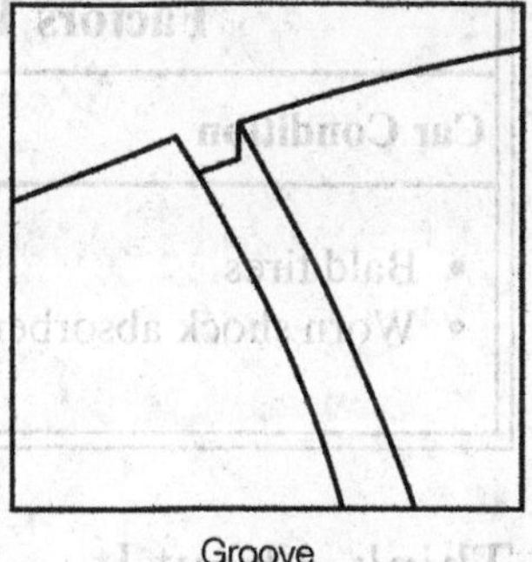

Words and Ideas

friction: Friction is the force that keeps the tires of your vehicle from sliding on the road.

traction: This is the ability of the tire to grip the road because of friction.

groove: A groove is a long, narrow cut. A tire that has grooves will have good traction.

Think About It

Below are listed six road conditions. Circle the conditions that would reduce traction and make it more difficult to stop your vehicle.

a. icy road　　**b.** gravel road　　**c.** dry road

d. wet leaves on road　　**e.** oil on the road　　**f.** rain

hydroplaning: When a vehicle is hydroplaning, it is out of control floating along the surface of a wet road.

tread: This is the outer grooved surface of a tire that grips the road.

bald tire: A bald tire is a smooth tire without tread. Bald tires are dangerous because they cannot grip a wet road.

Tire with tread

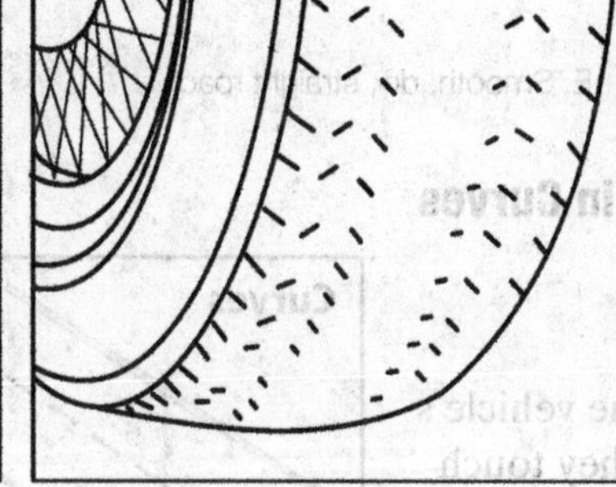
Bald tire

blowout: This is a sudden loss of tire air pressure while driving. After a blowout, your tire is flat. If your tire gets a blowout, it is very hard to steer.

puncture: A puncture happens when something pokes a hole in the tire.

underinflation: There is not enough air in your vehicle's tires when they are underinflated.

overinflation: There is too much air in your vehicle's tires when they are overinflated.

temperature: The temperature is how hot or cold—how many degrees—something is. You can use the Fahrenheit or the Celsius system to measure temperature.

Factors That Reduce Traction				
Car Condition	**Roadway Surface**		**Weather**	
• Bald tires • Worn shock absorbers	• wet • muddy • sandy	• gravel • oily • icy	• Rain • Snow	

Think About It

Below are pictures of six different road surface conditions. Circle the letters of the ones that provide less traction for your vehicle.

Road surface conditions

A. Curved road

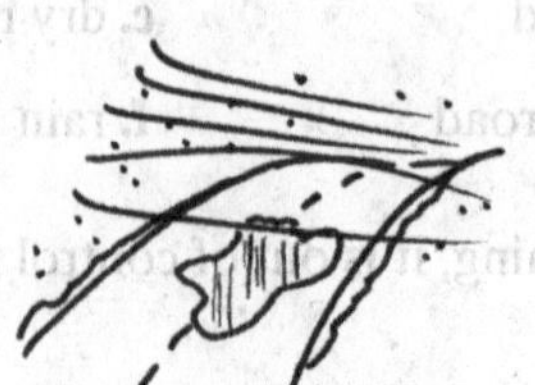

B. Icy road

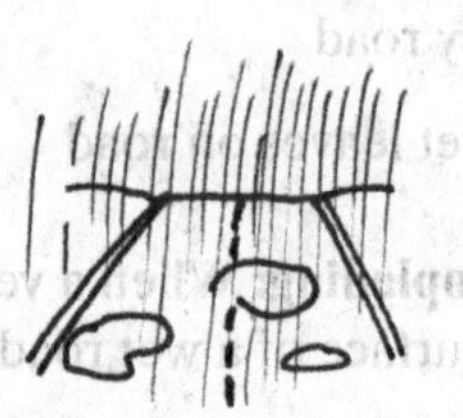

C. Wet road

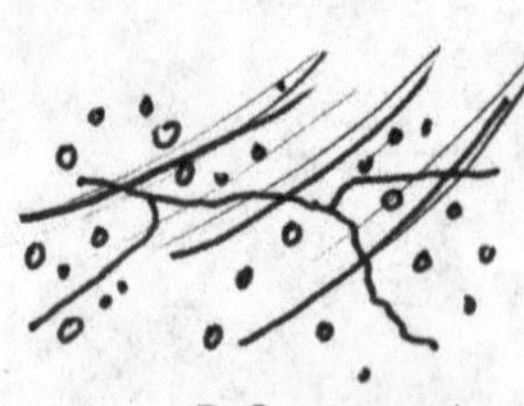

D. Snowy road

E. Smooth, dry, straight road

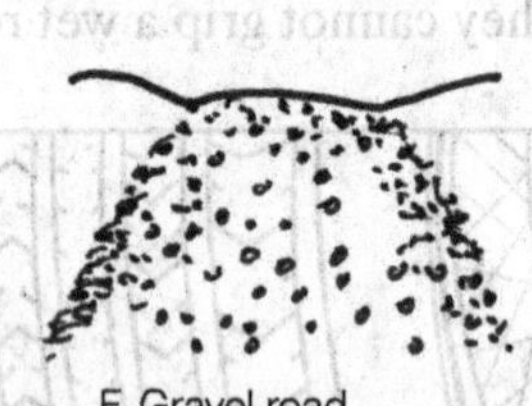

F. Gravel road

9.3 Vehicle Balance and Control in Curves

Words and Ideas

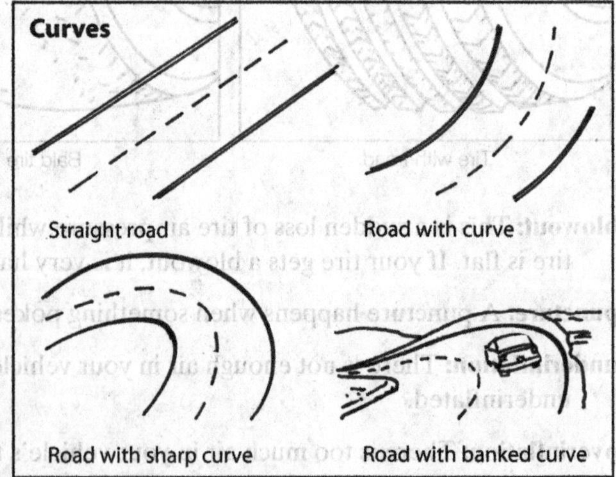

vehicle balance: This refers to the way the vehicle's weight is divided among its tires as they touch the ground.

pitch: Pitch is a movement in which a vehicle tilts from front to back, or back to front.

curve: A road that does not run in a straight line will have bends or curves on it.

banked curve: A curve that is higher on the outside than it is on the inside is called a banked curve. This type of curve helps your vehicle's tendency to move to the outside of the curve.

center of gravity: This is the point around which an object's weight is evenly distributed.

stability: This means steadiness. A vehicle's stability means it will stay upright.

load: The load is the amount of something a person or vehicle can carry.

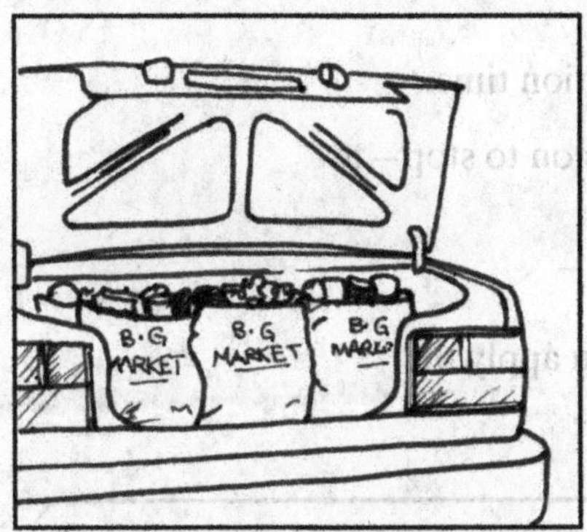

A load of groceries

A load of tools

Double Trouble

Some words have two or more meanings. Study the meanings of the following words.

stable: (1) a place to keep horses. **(2)** steady; not falling

square: (1) a mathematical term that means to multiply a number by itself. For example, "2 squared" means 2 × 2. **(2)** a geometric shape

square

bank: (1) a place to keep your money. **(2)** a term used to describe a curve; a banked curve is high on the outside and low on the inside.

Now, write 1 or 2 to show which meaning of each word is being used in the paragraph below.

On his way to the stable (a.______), Mr. Kim decided to stop at a store and buy a small table for the backyard. But first he had to stop at the bank (b.______) to get some money. He was looking for a square (c.______) table. He found one, but the table wasn't very stable (d.______). He was afraid the table would fall over. It was getting late. Mr. Kim had to go feed his horses. It had started to rain and the road had many curves. Fortunately, Mr. Kim had new tires on his car and the curves were banked (e.______) so it was easier to make the turns.

9.4 Stopping Distance

Words and Ideas

perceive: To perceive is to use your senses—especially sight and hearing—to become aware of something. When you perceive hazards in your path of travel, you are able to decide and evaluate what action to take.

total stopping distance: This is how far your vehicle travels while you make a stop. It begins when you first see something and realize you need to stop.

Name ______________________ Date ______________

perception time: This is the length of time it takes you to see a hazard and predict and decide the need to stop.

perception distance: This is how far your vehicle travels during perception time.

reaction time: This is the length of time you take to execute your decision to stop—to apply the brake.

reaction distance: This is how far your vehicle travels while you react.

braking distance: This is how far your vehicle travels from the time you apply the brake until your vehicle stops.

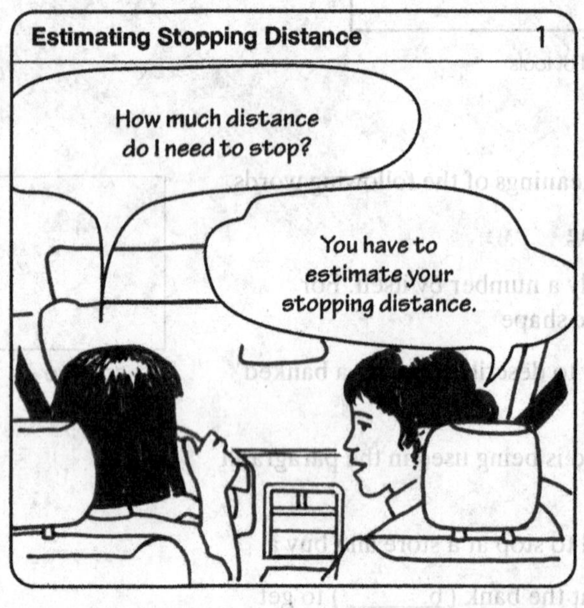

Name ______________________ Date ______________

9.5 Controlling Force of Impact

Words and Ideas

impact: Impact is when two things hit each other; a collision.

force of impact: This is the strength with which one moving object hits another object; this varies according to speed, weight, and distance between the impact and stop.

proportional: Proportional means having a constant ratio. Force of impact is proportional to the square of the increase of speed. When a car goes two times faster, it hits something four times harder. When a car goes three times faster, it hits something nine times harder.

restraint device: Restrain means to hold back. A restraint device is any part of a vehicle that holds an occupant in a collision.

passive restraint device: This is a restraint device that works automatically, such as an air bag. You do not have to do anything to make the device work.

active restraint device: This is a restraint device that you have to do something to make it work. You have to buckle or adjust a safety belt.

air bag: This is a balloon-type passive restraint device that automatically inflates—fills with air—to protect you.

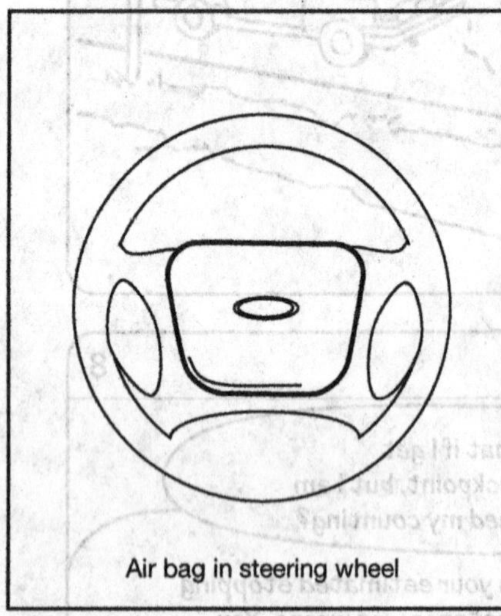
Air bag in steering wheel

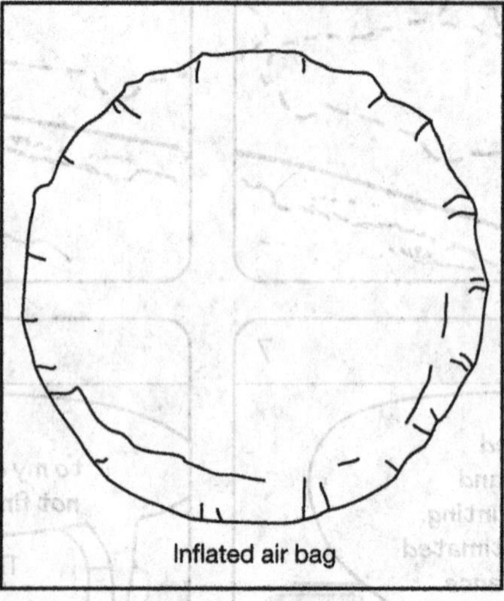
Inflated air bag

Think About It

Write *True* or *False* for each statement.

1. You can always stop your car in 4 seconds no matter how fast you are driving. ______________
2. It is harder to stop a car quickly on wet or gravelly roads. ______________
3. Only the driver of a vehicle needs to wear a safety belt. ______________
4. A loaded car will need more stopping distance than an empty car. ______________
5. Passengers in the back seat only need to wear safety belts on long trips. ______________

Name ______________________ Date ____________

Learning New Words

Take a look at Chapter 10 to familiarize yourself with the topics covered. Look for all the highlighted words in **dark** print. These are the vocabulary words. Write the words on a sheet of paper, then write the meaning next to each word.

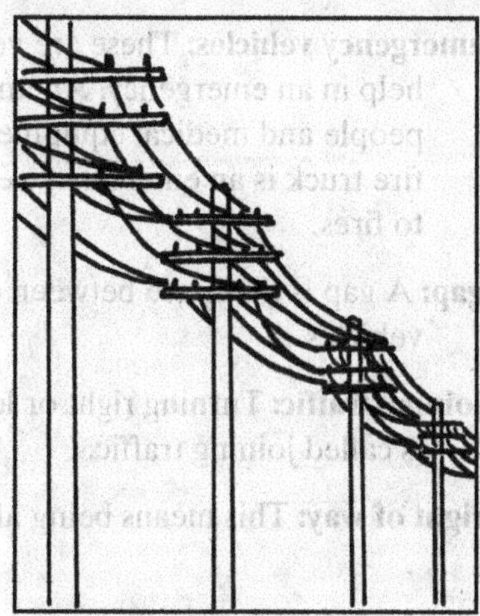

Power lines

10.1 Searching Intersections

Words and Ideas

power lines: Power lines are heavy electrical wires that carry electrical power to homes and businesses in the community.

point of no return: When you drive toward an intersection, this is the point beyond which you can no longer stop safely.

safety stop: This is a stop made with your front bumper even with the curb line, so you can search an intersection 90 degrees in both directions.

Figure It Out: Intersections

How can you tell that you are approaching an intersection? Look at the pictures below. For each picture, circle the items that indicate you are near an intersection. Write the names of these items in the space provided under each picture. Use *Drive Right* page 184 if you need help.

a. ______________________________

b. ______________________________

Name ______________________ Date ____________

10.2 Determining Right of Way and Judging Gaps

Words and Ideas

yield: This is letting others go first.

emergency vehicles: These are vehicles that carry people and equipment to help in an emergency. An ambulance is an emergency vehicle. It carries people and medical equipment to help people who are sick or injured. A fire truck is an emergency vehicle that carries fire fighters and equipment to fires.

Fire truck

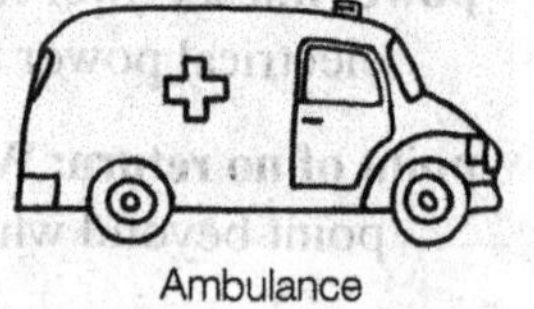

Ambulance

gap: A gap is the space between objects. In driving it is the distance between vehicles.

joining traffic: Turning right or left into lanes where other vehicles are traveling is called joining traffic.

right of way: This means being allowed to use a certain part of the roadway first.

Name ______________________ Date __________

10.3 Controlled Intersections

Words and Ideas

controlled intersection: A controlled intersection has traffic signals or signs to direct traffic.

Controlled Intersections

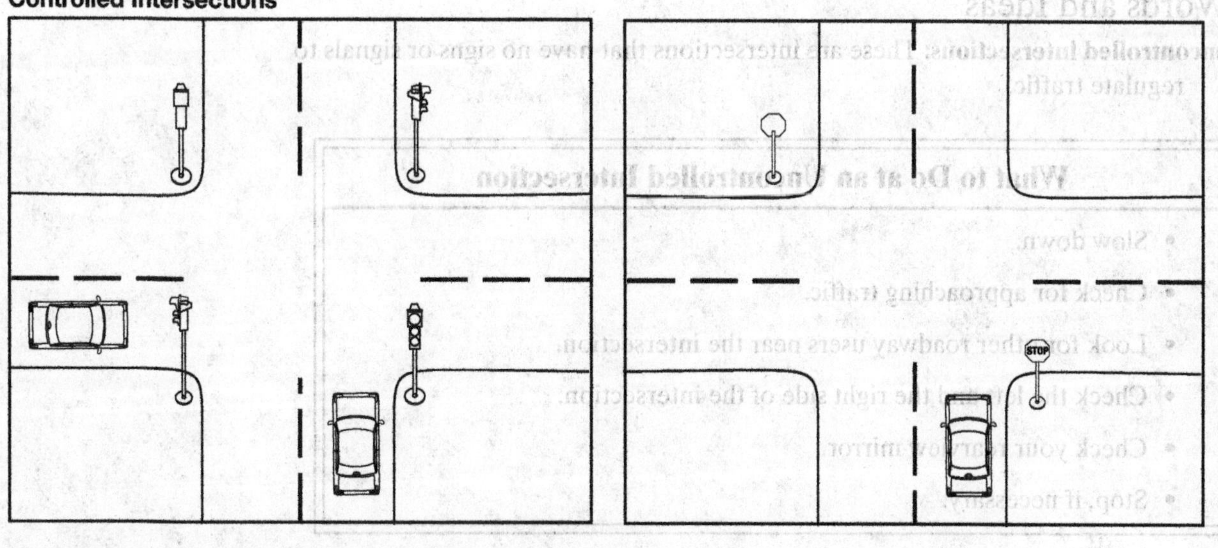

through street: A street without STOP signs, YIELD signs, or traffic signals is a through street. Drivers on the through street usually can go through an intersection without stopping.

stale green light: State means old. A stale green light is a traffic light that has been green for a long time.

fresh green light: Fresh means new. A fresh green light is a traffic light that has just turned from red to green.

protected left turn: Protect means to keep safe from danger. Some traffic signals protect a driver making a left turn with special signals.

unprotected left turn: An unprotected left turn is made without a special left turn light.

Left Turns	
Protected	Unprotected
• Special green arrow or light tells you when to turn. • Other traffic stops while you turn.	• There is no special light or arrow. • You must yield to oncoming traffic.

delayed green light: Sometimes one side of an intersection has a green light while the light for the oncoming traffic remains red.

10.4 Uncontrolled Intersections

Words and Ideas

uncontrolled intersections: These are intersections that have no signs or signals to regulate traffic.

What to Do at an Uncontrolled Intersection
• Slow down. • Check for approaching traffic. • Look for other roadway users near the intersection. • Check the left and the right side of the intersection. • Check your rearview mirror. • Stop, if necessary.

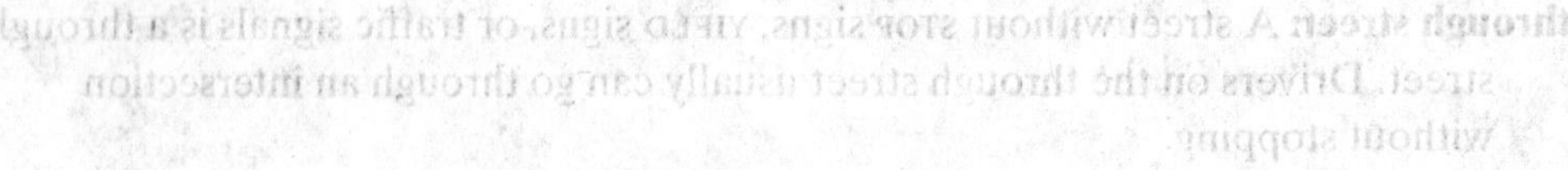

Name ______________________ Date ____________

update: To update is to add new information or make corrections.

location: Your location is the place where you are; your position.

Think About It: Uncontrolled Intersections

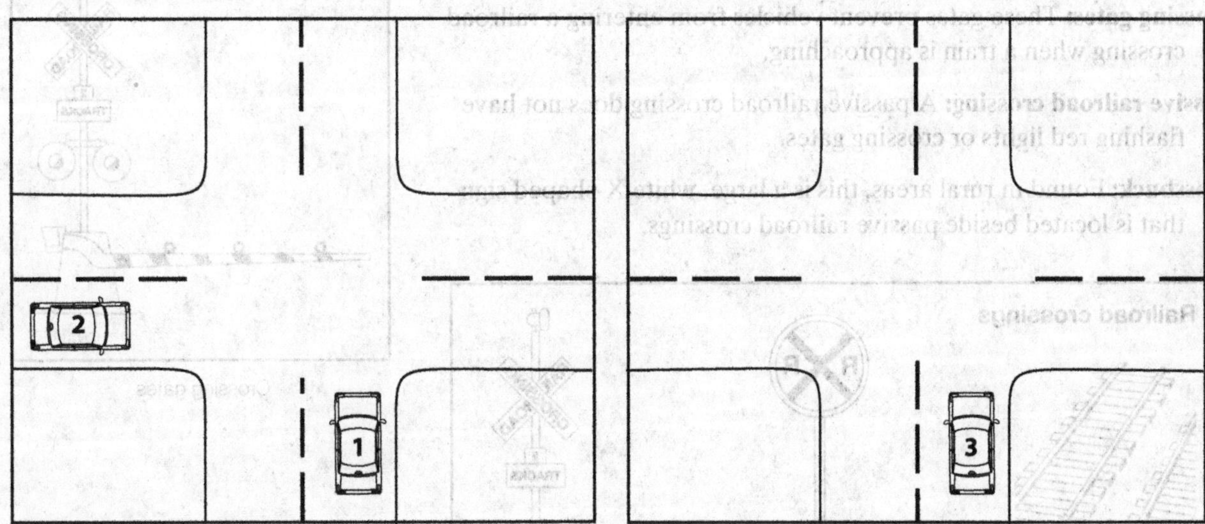

Read the statements below, then circle the letter next to the best answer.

1. You approach an uncontrolled intersection. You are driving car number 1 in the picture. Car number 2 is approaching the intersection at the same time.
   a. You assume you have the right of way and keep driving.
   b. You drive defensively. You stop at the intersection and give the other car the right of way.

2. You approach an empty, uncontrolled intersection. You are driving car number 3. You don't see any cars or other roadway users.
   a. You slow down as you get closer to the intersection. You continue looking for other roadway users.
   b. You continue driving at the same speed because the intersection is empty.

3. You are driving car number 3. As you approach an uncontrolled intersection, you see a pedestrian out of the corner of your eye.
   a. Accelerate to get through the intersection before the pedestrian.
   b. Stop, make eye contact, and use a hand signal to communicate to the pedestrian which one of you will yield.

10.5 Railroad Crossings

Words and Ideas

active railroad crossing: These railroad crossings are controlled by flashing red lights and/or crossing gates.

crossing gates: These gates prevent vehicles from entering a railroad crossing when a train is approaching.

passive railroad crossing: A passive railroad crossing does not have flashing red lights or crossing gates.

crossbuck: Found in rural areas, this is a large, white X-shaped sign that is located beside passive railroad crossings.

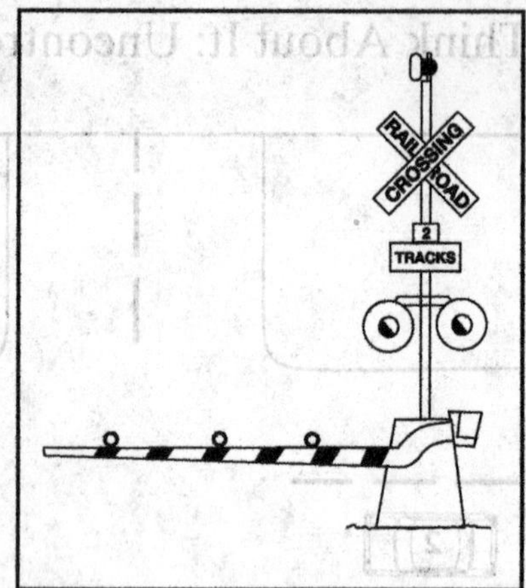

Crossing gates

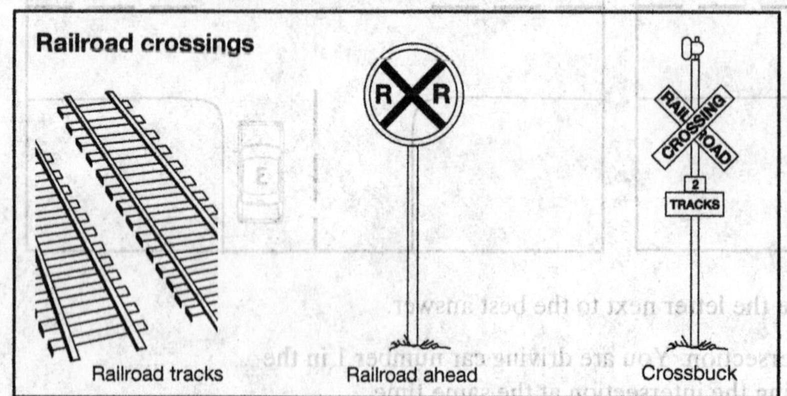

Name ______________________________ Date ____________

Think About It

Read the statements below, then circle the letter next to the best answer.

1. When you approach railroad tracks,
   a. you should always slow down, even if you don't see a train.
   b. you should slow down only if you see a train.

2. After a train has passed,
   a. drive across the tracks as quickly as possible.
   b. check the crossing to see if another train is approaching.

10.6 Roundabouts

Words and Ideas

roundabout: A roundabout is where several intersections meet and form a circle.

Think About It

Write *True* or *False* for each statement in the space provided.

1. Roundabouts are safer and more efficient than intersections with traffic signals. ________________

2. Vehicles traveling in a roundabout must yield the right of way to newcomers. ________________

3. Never stop in a traffic circle. ________________

4. Do not pass or change lanes except to merge into the right lane to exit. ________________

Learning New Words

Take a look at Chapter 11 to familiarize yourself with the topics covered. Look for all the highlighted words in **dark** print. These are the vocabulary words. Write the words on a sheet of paper, then write the meaning next to each word.

11.1 Pedestrians

Words and Ideas

pedestrians: Pedestrians are people who are using roadways and are not in vehicles. Pedestrians may be walking or running.

vulnerable: To be vulnerable is to be easily hurt.

jaywalk: When pedestrians do not follow traffic rules and signals, they are jaywalking.

moral: To be moral is to do the right thing.

legal: To be legal is to follow laws.

obligation: Your obligation is what you must do.

moral and legal obligation: Your obligation is to protect pedestrians because it is the right and lawful thing to do.

alley: This is a narrow street or passageway between buildings or other structures that may make it difficult to see pedestrians or moving vehicles.

business districts: Business districts are areas where there are many stores and other places of business.

residential areas: Residential areas are areas where there are homes where people live.

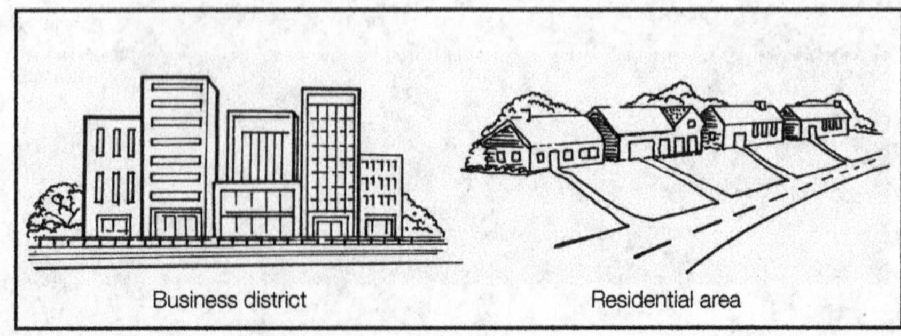

Name ______________________________ Date ______________

11.2 Bicycles and Mopeds

Words and Ideas

headphones: Headphones are devices that fit in your ears and allow you to listen to the radio or other audio players.

hand-operated brakes: Bicycle brakes are operated with your hands—hand-operated brakes.

moped: A moped is a two-wheeled vehicle that can be driven with either a motor or a pedal.

restrictions: To restrict is to keep within limits. Moped and motor scooter riders have restrictions against driving on certain high-speed roadways.

hand throttle: The hand throttle on a motorcycle is like the accelerator on a car.

swerve: To swerve is to turn away from a straight course.

tape: Tape is a narrow strip of strong woven fabric or plastic that is sticky on one side.

reflective tape: This is special tape that becomes very bright when light shines on it at night.

Figure It Out: Bicycle Hazards

Look at the picture below. Find four hazards for the bicyclist. List the hazards on the lines provided.

1. ______________________________
2. ______________________________
3. ______________________________
4. ______________________________

Name ______________________________ Date ______________

11.3 Motorcycles and Scooters

Words and Ideas

motorcyclist: A person riding a motorcycle is called a motorcyclist.

scooter: A scooter is a low-powered, two-wheeled vehicle that is more powerful than a moped.

major: Major is important; a large part.

share: To share is to take part of something and to allow someone else to have the other part.

alert: To be alert is to be ready to see and hear what is going on around you.

crucial: The Identify step is crucial—extremely important—for drivers because motorcycles are more difficult to see than larger vehicles.

Think About It

Look at the vehicles below. Which one is the hardest to see? Which one is the easiest to see? Put the pictures in order. Write the number 1 under the vehicle that is the hardest to see. As the numbers increase, the vehicle is easier to see. The vehicle easiest to see is number 5.

a. ______________________

b. ______________________

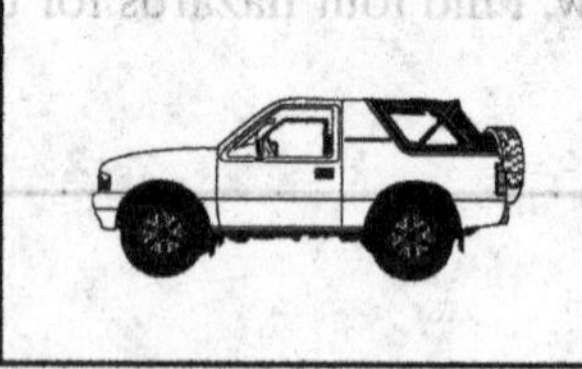

c. ______________________

d. ______________________

e. ______________________

Name ______________________ Date ____________

stability: Stability means ability to stay in position. Vehicles with four tires on the road have more stability than motorcycles that only have two tires on the road.

Motorcycles and Cars: Sharing the Responsibility

Think About It

Read the statements below. Write *True* or *False* for each statement.

1. Cars and motorcycles have the same brake system. ____________
2. Motorcycles and cars have the same number of headlights. ____________
3. Motorcycle taillights are as easy to see as car taillights. ____________
4. A motorcyclist is less protected than the driver of a vehicle. ____________

Headlight
Handlebar
Taillights

Motorcycle

anticipate: To anticipate is to feel or realize something before it happens.

protective gear: These are items a motorcyclist wears to protect the head, eyes, and body.

helmet: This is worn on the heads of motorcyclists to protect them from head injuries.

goggles: Goggles are like glasses, but they are worn to protect the motorcyclist's eyes.

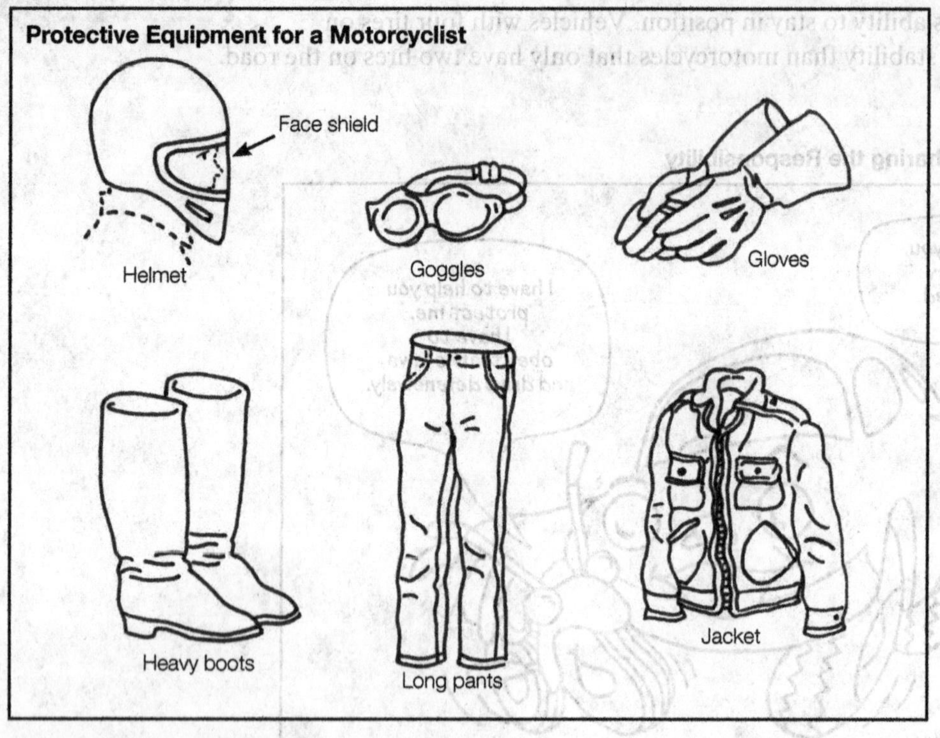

adverse weather: Rain, sleet, ice, snow, and other weather conditions that make driving hazardous are adverse weather conditions. Adverse weather conditions are much more difficult for motorcyclists than for other drivers.

offset position: Motorcyclists should ride in an offset position—not in a line—so that one rider is slightly behind and to the side of the other.

visible: To be more visible is to be seen better. Motorcyclists need to be seen by other drivers.

Name ______________________ Date ____________

11.4 Trucks, Buses, and Emergency and Specialized Vehicles

Words and Ideas

snowplows: Snowplows are big trucks that remove the snow from the roadways.

emergency vehicles: These are vehicles that respond to emergency situations. They carry police officers, fire fighters, paramedics, and other emergency personnel.

sirens: Emergency vehicles have loud, wailing sirens to warn drivers. Always pull to the right and let emergency vehicles pass.

Figure It Out

Read the following statements, then circle the letter next to the correct answer.

1. When you approach a school bus with yellow lights flashing, you should
   a. pass on the right.
   b. stop.
   c. wave to the students as you drive past.

2. When an emergency vehicle with lights flashing approaches you, you should
   a. pull to the right.
   b. go faster and try to outrun the emergency vehicle.
   c. do nothing.

Think About It

Write *True* or *False* after each statement.

1. Emergency vehicles use their sirens and lights only during emergencies. ________________

2. When emergency vehicles go to an emergency, they always have the right of way. ________________

trailer: This is a large transport container that is designed to be hauled by a truck.

tractor-trailer: This is a truck that has a tractor—cab and motor—that pulls a separate trailer.

semi-trailer: This is a type of tractor-trailer that pulls one trailer; commonly called an "eighteen wheeler."

no zones: These are large blind-spot areas where truck drivers cannot see other vehicles.

wind gust: When passing a large truck, you might experience a wind gust—a sudden rush of wind.

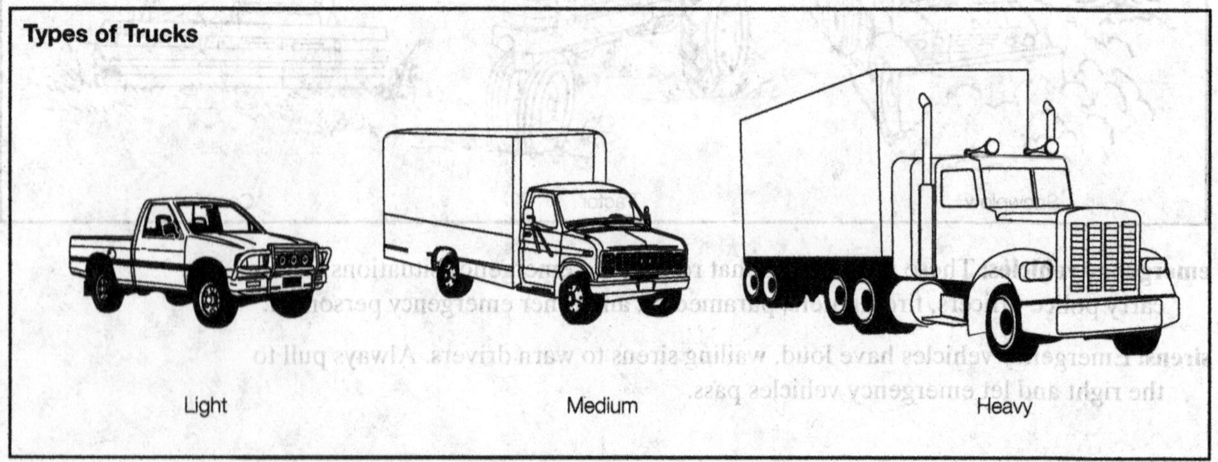

low-speed vehicles (LSVs): These are four-wheeled vehicles with top speeds between 20 and 25 mph.

neighborhood electric vehicles (NEVs): These are low-speed vehicles that run on electricity.

Name ______________________ Date __________

Learning New Words

Take a look at Chapter 12 to familiarize yourself with the topics covered. Look for all the highlighted words in **dark** print. These are the vocabulary words. Write each word on a sheet of paper, then write the meaning next to the word.

12.1 Reduced Visibility

Words and Ideas

reduced visibility: When your visibility is reduced, your ability to see is less. Your visibility can be reduced by problems with your car's windows, time of day, and bad weather.

moisture: Moisture is wetness. When something is moist, it is damp.

front-window defroster: This is part of the heating system in your vehicle. The window defroster sends warm, dry air to the windshield. The warm, dry air will remove frost and steam.

rear defogger: These are small bands across the rear window that allow you to clear the rear window of frost and steam. This is often a separate switch on the instrument panel.

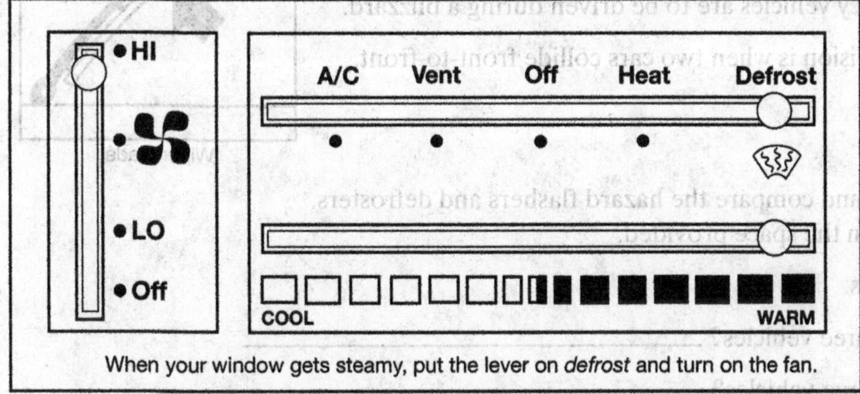

When your window gets steamy, put the lever on *defrost* and turn on the fan.

glare: To glare is to shine intensely and blindingly. When there is sun glare, your visibility is reduced.

sun visor: Above the windshield on the driver's side and the passenger's side are pulldown sun visors. These will help shield your eyes from sun glare.

low-beam headlights: When you turn on your headlights, they are aimed low on the roadway and are low-beam.

high-beam headlights: To see farther ahead on a rural road, use high-beam headlights that are aimed high on the roadway. Switch to low-beam when an oncoming car approaches you.

flick your headlights: To flick means to turn on and off or to switch. You can flick from low-beam to high-beam headlights to signal to other drivers to use their low-beam headlights.

overdriving headlights: Driving at a speed at which the part of the road lighted by your headlights is not as far as the distance needed to stop your vehicle is called overdriving headlights.

industrial smoke: This is heavy smoke that is released into the air by factories and other plants. Industrial smoke can be very dense and dangerous to drive through because of the loss of visibility.

Driving in Fog, Rain, and Snow
• Use low-beam headlights. • Slow down. • Look for any problems. • Make your space cushion larger. • If you pull off the road, use your hazard flashers.

windshield wipers: Windshield wipers keep your vehicle windshield clear of rain, sleet, and snow.

wind-driven snow: This is snow that the wind blows across the road.

slush: Wet, icy snow is called slush.

blizzard: A blizzard is a very big snowstorm with strong wind and heavy snow. In most states, only emergency vehicles are to be driven during a blizzard.

head-on collision: A head-on collision is when two cars collide front-to-front.

Wiper blade

Figure It Out

Look at three different vehicles, and compare the hazard flashers and defrosters. Answer the following questions in the space provided.

1. Locate the emergency flashers.

Does it look the same in all three vehicles? ______________________

Is it in the same place in all three vehicles? ______________________

2. Locate the defrost symbol.

Does the symbol look the same in each vehicle? ______________________

Is it in the same place in each vehicle? ______________________

12.2 Reduced Traction

Words and Ideas

hydroplaning: This occurs when your vehicle rides on top of water and the tires no longer have contact with the road.

combination: A combination is when two or more things are mixed together.

standing water: Water that is not moving, such as a puddle, is standing water.

tire chains: These are chains that fit around tires to give them more traction on roads that are slippery because of snow. Chains may be required in some mountain roads when it snows.

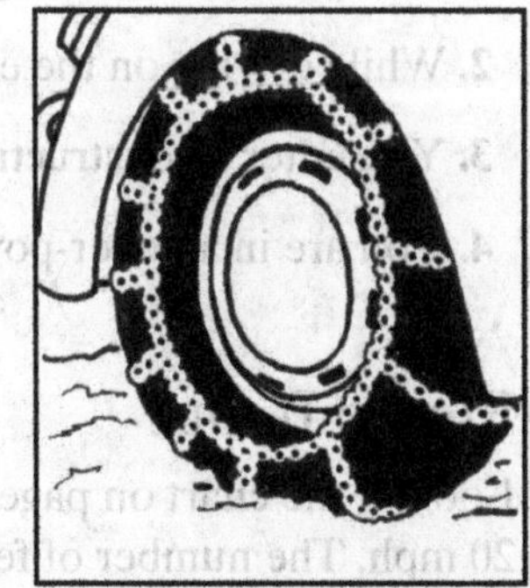

Tire chains

rocking a vehicle: If your vehicle gets stuck in deep snow, mud, or sand, this is a method to get out. Repeat the sequence of driving forward a little and then back a little—rock the vehicle.

Rocking back and forth to get out of the snow

spin: This is when the tires are turning, but the vehicle is not able to move in any direction.

sleet: This is a frozen rain; rain that is mixed with snow.

squeeze: To squeeze your brakes is to step on them lightly until they just begin to work. This is a way to check traction on icy roads.

overpasses: Overpasses are bridges or roads that pass over another road.

black ice: This is ice that forms in thin sheets. Black ice is very difficult to see.

marbles: These are small, round glass balls. Gravel can act like marbles under the tires of your vehicle and cause skids.

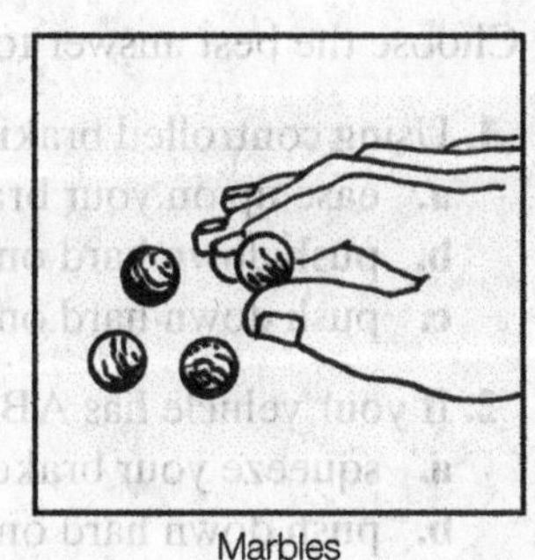

Marbles

skid: When you skid, your vehicle loses part or all of its grip on the road.

understeer situation: This is a result of your vehicle not turning enough.

oversteer situation: This is a result of your vehicle turning too sharply.

fishtail: Fishtail is when the rear end of a vehicle slides from side to side.

Name ______________________________ Date ______________

Think About It

In each of the following situations, decide if you should

- **a.** press down on the accelerator to speed up, or
- **b.** let up on the accelerator to slow down, or
- **c.** step on the brake.

1. You must drive through standing water. __
2. While driving on the expressway, you see ice patches on the road ahead. __
3. You enter a construction area and see sand in the road. __
4. You are in an over-power skid and begin to spin. __

Figure It Out

Look at the chart on page 241 of *Drive Right.* In each situation, the cars are driving at 20 mph. The number of feet tells you how long it takes each car to stop after braking. If you are driving on a snow-packed road and your tires have reinforced chains, it will take you 38 feet to stop. Use the space provided to write your answers.
Now use the chart to answer the following questions:

1. On which road surface will it take the longest to stop? ______________________

____

2. On which road do you have the best traction with conventional tires? __________

____

3. Compared to dry concrete, how many more feet do you need to stop on packed snow with conventional tires? ______________________

____

controlled braking: This is a method for reducing your speed as quickly as possible without losing steering control of your vehicle.

locking your wheels: When your wheels lock, they cannot roll, and the vehicle may skid.

Think About It

Choose the best answer to complete each sentence below.

1. Using controlled braking when your wheels lock without ABS, you should
   - **a.** ease up on your brake pedal and then squeeze the brakes.
   - **b.** push down hard on the accelerator.
   - **c.** push down hard on your brakes.
2. If your vehicle has ABS and you need to stop suddenly, you should
   - **a.** squeeze your brakes.
   - **b.** push down hard on your brakes.
   - **c.** use your emergency brake.

Name ______________________________ Date ______________

12.3 Other Adverse Weather Conditions

Words and Ideas

blast of wind: This is a sudden, strong wind.

crosswinds: These are winds that blow across your vehicle.

tornado: This is a violent storm that produces funnel-like destructive winds.

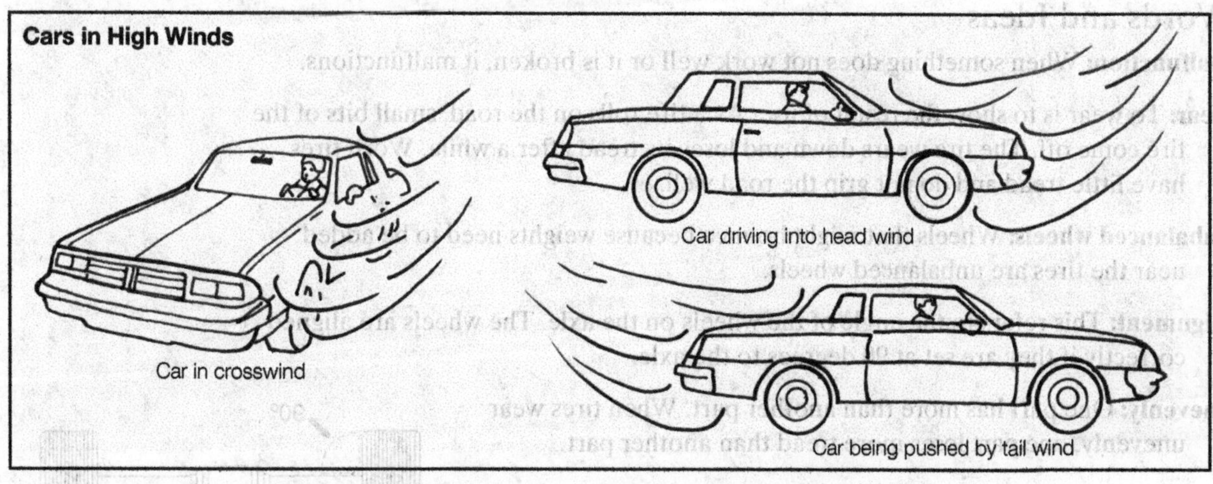

scald: This is to burn by hot liquid or steam. The radiator in your vehicle contains water. When the engine overheats—gets too hot—the water may turn to steam. If you open the radiator when the engine is hot, the steam will come out and scald you.

exhaust pipe: The exhaust pipe, or tailpipe, is the pipe at the rear of a vehicle that exhaust gases come out of.

racing the engine: This is stepping on the accelerator pedal to make the engine run fast while the car is not moving.

stalled: Drivers who are stalled are drivers whose vehicles are not running due to adverse weather or mechanical conditions. Stalled vehicles may be in your path of travel during severe storms.

Think About It

Write *True* or *False* next to each statement.

1. You will need to make steering corrections for crosswinds. ______________

2. If you see a tornado, stay in your car. ______________

3. If you are stuck in snow with your engine running, make sure the exhaust pipe is not blocked. ______________

4. When your car's engine is cold, you should race it. ______________

5. Winter driving is usually easier than summer driving. ______________

Name ______________________ Date ____________

Learning New Words

Take a look at Chapter 13 to familiarize yourself with the topics covered. Look for all the highlighted words in **dark** print. These are the vocabulary words. Write each word on a sheet of paper, then write the meaning next to the word.

13.1 Vehicle Malfunctions

Words and Ideas

malfunction: When something does not work well or it is broken, it malfunctions.

wear: To wear is to show the result of use. As a tire rolls on the road, small bits of the tire come off. The tire wears down and loses its tread after a while. Worn tires have little tread and do not grip the road well.

unbalanced wheels: Wheels that might bounce because weights need to be added near the tires are unbalanced wheels.

alignment: This refers to the angle of the wheels on the axle. The wheels are aligned correctly if they are set at 90 degrees to the axle.

unevenly: One part has more than another part. When tires wear unevenly, one part loses more tread than another part.

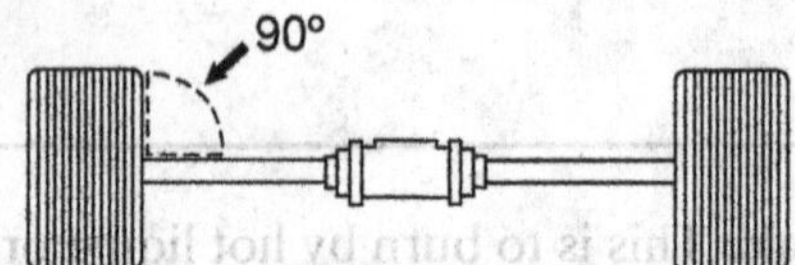

Aligned Wheels

blowout: This is a sudden flat tire while you are driving.

fishtailing: This is the back and forth swerving of the rear of a vehicle. If your vehicle has a blowout, it might fishtail.

When Your Tire Blows Out

- Grip the steering wheel firmly.
- Take your foot off the accelerator, but do not brake.
- Check traffic.
- Drive off the road slowly, braking gently.
- Turn on the hazard flashers. Drive slowly until you find a safe place to stop.

spare tire: The extra tire in the trunk of your vehicle—or attached to the back with some vehicles—is called a spare tire. This tire can be used in case you have a flat tire or a blowout. You should always have a good spare tire in your vehicle.

compact spare: A spare tire that is meant to be temporary. Compact spares are usually smaller than regular tires.

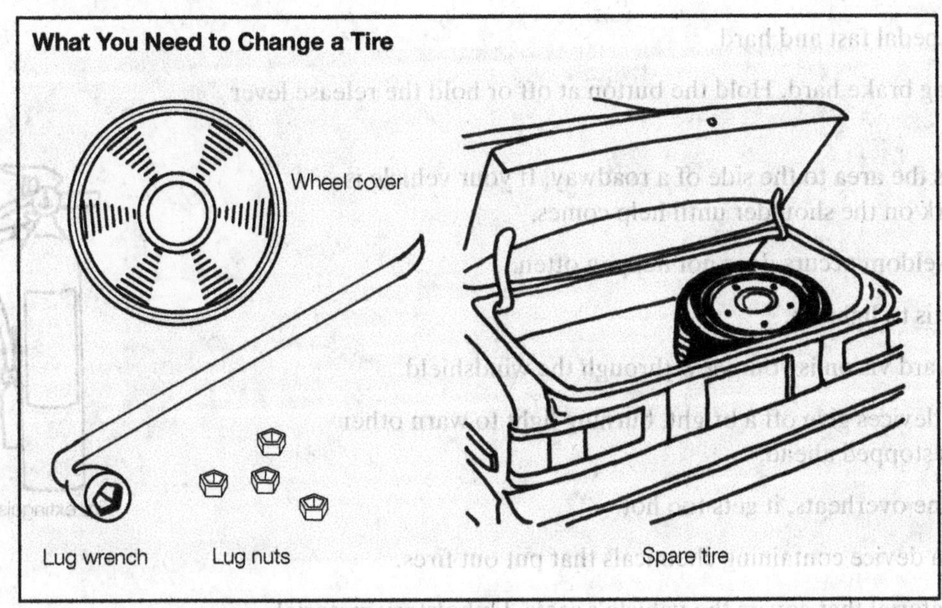

brake warning light: This is the light that comes on when part of your braking system is not working.

brake fade: This is when brakes don't work well. Brake fade is caused by overheating of the brakes after long, continuous, hard braking.

parking brake: This is a separate braking system from your main braking system. The parking brake holds your vehicle when it is parked. Some parking brakes are an extra foot pedal to the left side of the other pedals. Others are a lever you pull by hand.

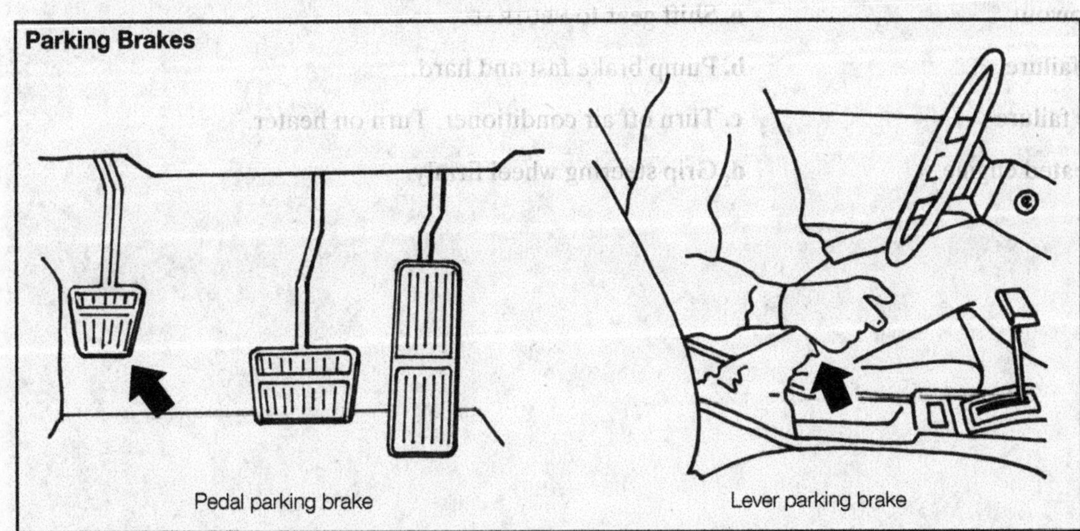

Figure It Out: Brake Failure

What should you do in case of a total brake failure? You must follow four steps. Read the four steps below and add a number to show the correct order. If you need help, turn to page 252 in *Drive Right*.

__ **A.** Search for an open zone.

__ **B.** Downshift to the lowest gear.

__ **C.** Pump the brake pedal fast and hard.

__ **D.** Apply the parking brake hard. Hold the button at off or hold the release lever out.

shoulder: The shoulder is the area to the side of a roadway. If your vehicle is disabled, you can park on the shoulder until help comes.

seldom: Something that seldom occurs does not happen often.

illuminate: To illuminate is to light up.

foward vision: Your forward vision is your view through the windshield.

flares: These emergency devices give off a bright, burning light to warn other motorists a vehicle is stopped ahead.

overheats: When an engine overheats, it gets too hot.

fire extinguisher: This is a device containing chemicals that put out fires.

upholstery: This is the material that covers the vehicle's seats. Upholstery material includes cloth, vinyl, and leather.

Fire extinguisher

Figure It Out: Emergencies

1. Column A lists several emergency situations. Column B lists first steps you should take in an emergency. Match the first steps to the situation. Write the correct answers in the space provided.

A: Emergencies	**B: First Steps**
__ **1.** tire blowout	**a.** Shift gear to NEUTRAL.
__ **2.** brake failure	**b.** Pump brake fast and hard.
__ **3.** engine failure	**c.** Turn off air conditioner. Turn on heater.
__ **4.** overheated engine	**d.** Grip steering wheel firmly.

Name ______________________________ Date ______________

Think About It

Read the statements below. Circle the letter next to the best answer.

1. During any kind of vehicle malfunction, you should
   a. pull off the road immediately.
   b. use your hazard flashers, horn, and hand signals to let other drivers know your condition while you prepare to pull off the road safely.
   c. continue driving until you get to a phone or service station.

2. If your car stops on the road and you cannot move it, you should
   a. turn on the hazard flashers, raise the hood, and wait in the car until help arrives.
   b. turn on the hazard flashers, raise the hood, get out of the car, and try to stop cars as they go by.
   c. turn on the hazard flashers, raise the hood, get out of the car, and walk to the nearest gas station.

3. If your engine overheats, you should
   a. turn on the air conditioner.
   b. turn on the heater.
   c. roll down the windows.

13.2 Driver Errors

Words and Ideas

driver errors: These are mistakes that drivers make.

drop off: This is a sudden difference in the level of the road between a higher road surface and a lower shoulder surface.

swerve: To swerve is to turn the wheel sharply so the vehicle changes paths quickly. You should only swerve in emergency situations when it is not safe to stop.

grade: Grade is the slope or slant of a road.

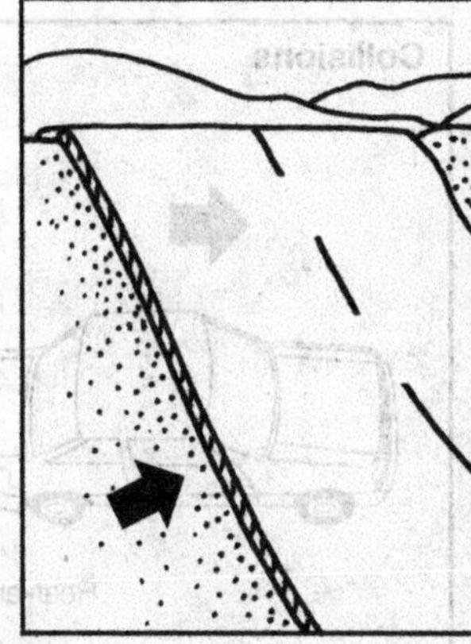

Drop off

13.3 Roadway Hazards

Words and Ideas

potholes: Holes in the roadway. Potholes can damage tires.

equalize: This means to make equal. Once the pressure is equalized in a vehicle that has gone into deep water, you can then open the door.

brief: Brief means short, little. *Example:* Since we only had five minutes before the game started, the coach gave us a brief talk.

air pocket: A pocket is a small, closed-in space. An air pocket is a small air-filled space trapped in the highest point of a vehicle for a short time after it sinks underwater.

1. If you cannot avoid a pothole, why should you drive slowly over the pothole? Give two reasons.

____

____

2. If you cannot open a window when your vehicle is in deep water, what should you do?

____

____

13.4 Collisions

Words and Ideas

minimize: The best way to minimize, or lessen, the impact of a collision is to keep control of your vehicle.

witnesses: These are people who saw the collision and can report what happened.

head-on collision: This is when the front of one car hits the front of another.

rear-end collision: A rear-end collision is when one car crashes into the back of another car traveling in the same direction.

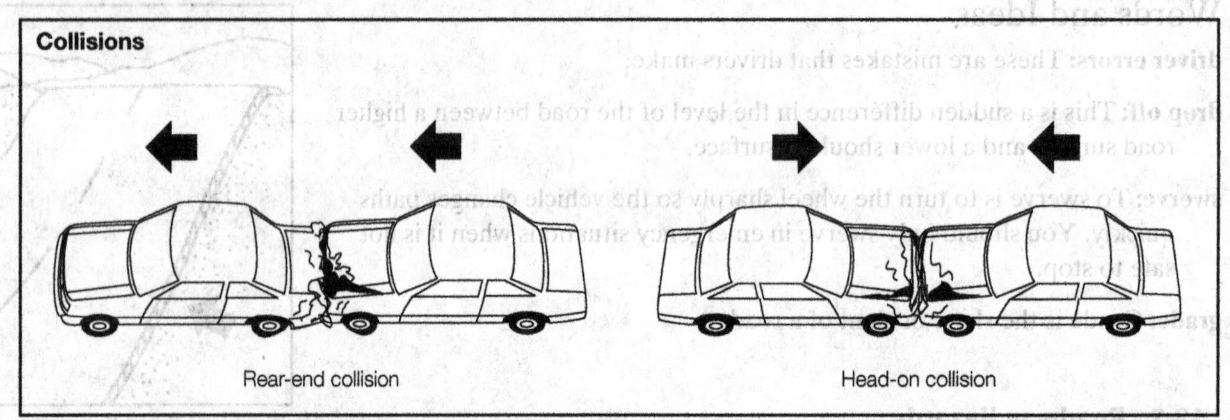

side-impact collision: This means getting hit on the side of your car.

offense: An offense is an illegal action. For example, driving when you are drunk is a very serious offense.

to aid: To aid means to help.

paramedics: Paramedics are specially trained people who can give medical help during emergencies such as collisions or fires. Paramedics are not doctors, but they know what to do during medical emergencies. Some paramedics are called *emergency medical technicians*.

to administer: To administer means to give.

to note: To note means to write down to help you remember.

proof of financial responsibility: This is something that shows you can pay for damages. An insurance card is one way to show proof of financial responsibility.

to notify: To notify means to let someone know, to tell.

promptly: Promptly means quickly.

Figure It Out

Use pages 265 and 266 in *Drive Right* to answer the questions.

1. What are two of the first things you should do if you have a collision?

____

____

2. If you are in a collision, what information should you get from each driver involved in the collision? List five things.

____

____

____

____

____

Think About It

Which type of collision can cause the most serious injuries? Why?

____

____

13.5 Insurance

Words and Ideas

financial responsibility law: This law requires you to prove that you can pay for damages you cause that result in death, injury, or property damage.

premium: This is the specific amount of money you pay for insurance coverage over a specified period of time.

policy: A policy is a written contract between an insured person and the insurance company that explains the terms of the insurance coverage.

liability insurance: This insurance provides money to another person because of injury or damage you cause.

bodily-injury insurance: This protects the driver who is at fault in a collision against all claims for injury to other people.

claims: This is a formal request for payments related to injuries to other people or damage to property belonging to others.

property-damage insurance: This protects the driver who is at fault in a collision against claims for damages to another person's property, up to specified limits.

medical-payment insurance: This insurance pays medical and funeral expenses for people injured or killed in an insured vehicle that is in a collision.

no-fault insurance: This covers an insured person's losses and expenses associated with the collision regardless of who is at fault.

collision insurance: This provides coverage to pay the costs of repair or replacement of your vehicle, less selected deductible.

deductible: This is the amount you agree to pay toward the repair or replacement of your vehicle. The amount of the deductible is stated in your insurance policy.

comprehensive insurance: This provides coverage for replacement or repair of your vehicle for damage caused by something other than a collision.

uninsured motorist insurance: This covers costs for damage or injury to you and your passengers if you are struck by another vehicle whose driver has no insurance.

underinsured motorist insurance: This covers the costs that another person's insurance company does not pay as a result of a collision.

Figure It Out: Insuring a Vehicle

In the box below, cross out the words or terms that do not belong with the idea of car insurance. Look at pages 267–270 in *Drive Right* if you need help.

Vehicle Insurance		
premium	loan	financial responsibility
interest	liability	uninsured motorist
warranty	claims	property damage
principal driver	high-risk driver	depreciation

Name ______________________ Date ______________

Learning New Words

Take a look at Chapter 14 to familiarize yourself with the topics covered. Look for all the highlighted words in **dark** print. These are the vocabulary words. Write the words on a sheet of paper, then write the meaning next to each word.

14.1 Adjusting to City Traffic

Words and Ideas

complexity: The complexity of a situation is how complex—how involved or difficult—it is.

dense: Dense traffic is heavy traffic.

traffic density: Traffic density is the measurement of how heavy traffic is.

attention: Attention is thinking about something or listening carefully to someone. When you give your attention to driving, you think about what you are doing. You watch and listen for vehicles, pedestrians, and other distractions.

City Driving

City driving requires your full attention. There is heavy traffic, and there are many distractions.

distraction: A distraction is something that takes your attention away. A radio, cellular phone, or other distractions take your attention away from driving.

cellular phone: Cellular phones are phones that run off a battery and can be used in vehicles. Do not use a cellular phone while driving.

Figure It Out: Driving Distractions

The pictures below show distractions. Circle the ones that distract you from driving safely.

Drink

Food

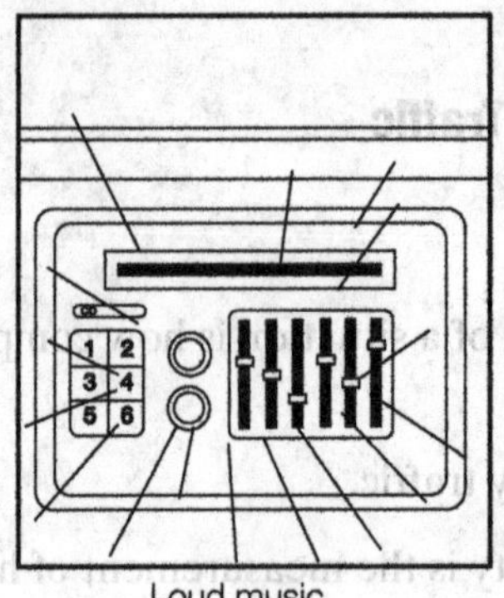
Loud music

Talking passenger

14.2 Following and Meeting Traffic

Words and Ideas

ample: Ample means enough. A 3-second following distance provides enough space around your vehicle for safe driving.

following distance: This is the space between you and the vehicle in front of you.

3-second following distance: This is a space between you and the vehicle in front of you that would take three seconds to cross at the speed you are travelling.

tailgate: To tailgate is to follow another vehicle too closely.

tailgater: A tailgater is a driver who follows another vehicle too closely.

flash your brake lights: Tapping your brake pedal causes the brake lights to flash—go on and off. Tap the brake pedal several times to warn the vehicle behind you that you are planning to stop or slow down.

Name ______________________________ Date ______________

Think About It

Look at the picture below, then answer the questions in the space provided.

Tailgating is Dangerous

a. b. c. d.

1. Which vehicle is tailgating? ______________________________
2. Which vehicle is being tailgated? ______________________________
3. Which vehicle is in the most danger? ______________________________

Think About It

Write *True* or *False* after each statement. If the statement is false, change the part that is wrong. Make the statement true.

1. It is raining very hard. You should keep the same following distance as usual.

   ____

2. You are in an unfamiliar neighborhood. You should slow down and look more carefully for possible hazards. ______________________________
3. Someone is tailgating you. You should speed up to increase the distance between you and the tailgater. ______________________________

Name ______________________________ Date ______________

14.3 Managing Space in City Traffic

Words and Ideas

cover the brake: When you cover the brake, you take your foot off the accelerator and hold it over the brake pedal to be ready to brake quickly.

ride the brake: When you ride the brake, you rest your foot on the brake. When you cover the brake, make sure you do not ride the brake.

overtake: When you overtake a vehicle, you pass that vehicle.

carpool, carpooling: When several people go to the same place in the same vehicle, it is called carpooling. If you and two of your friends ride to school together, you have a carpool.

High-Occupancy Vehicle (HOV) lanes: To help move rush-hour traffic, many cities have special lanes for carpools.

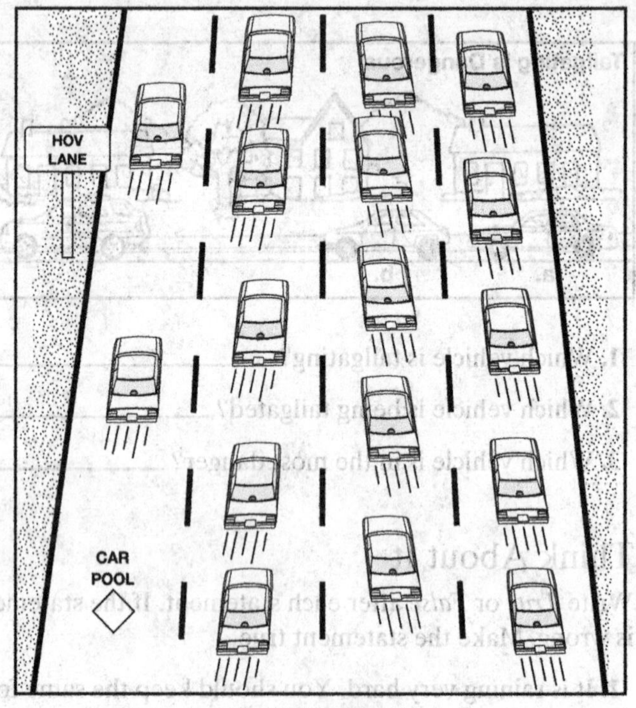

HOV lane

Think About It

Read each of the following situations. On the line after each situation, write yes if you should be covering your brake. Write no if you should not be covering your brake.

1. You are driving down a street with parked cars on both sides. ______________
2. You are driving on an expressway. Traffic is moving smoothly. ______________
3. You are driving on an expressway. In the distance, you see brake lights on the cars ahead of you. ______________
4. You are driving on a city street. You see children playing near the street. ________

Think About It: Riding Your Brake

Why it is bad to ride your brakes? ______________________________

____

Name ______________________ Date ____________

14.4 Special City Situations

Words and Ideas

blind intersection: This is an intersection where something blocks your view.

congested: Crowded streets that are clogged with traffic are congested streets.

one-way street: This is a street where all traffic goes in the same direction.

Figure It Out: One-Way Streets

Look at the picture below. Find four clues that tell you this is a one-way street. Write the clues on the lines provided.

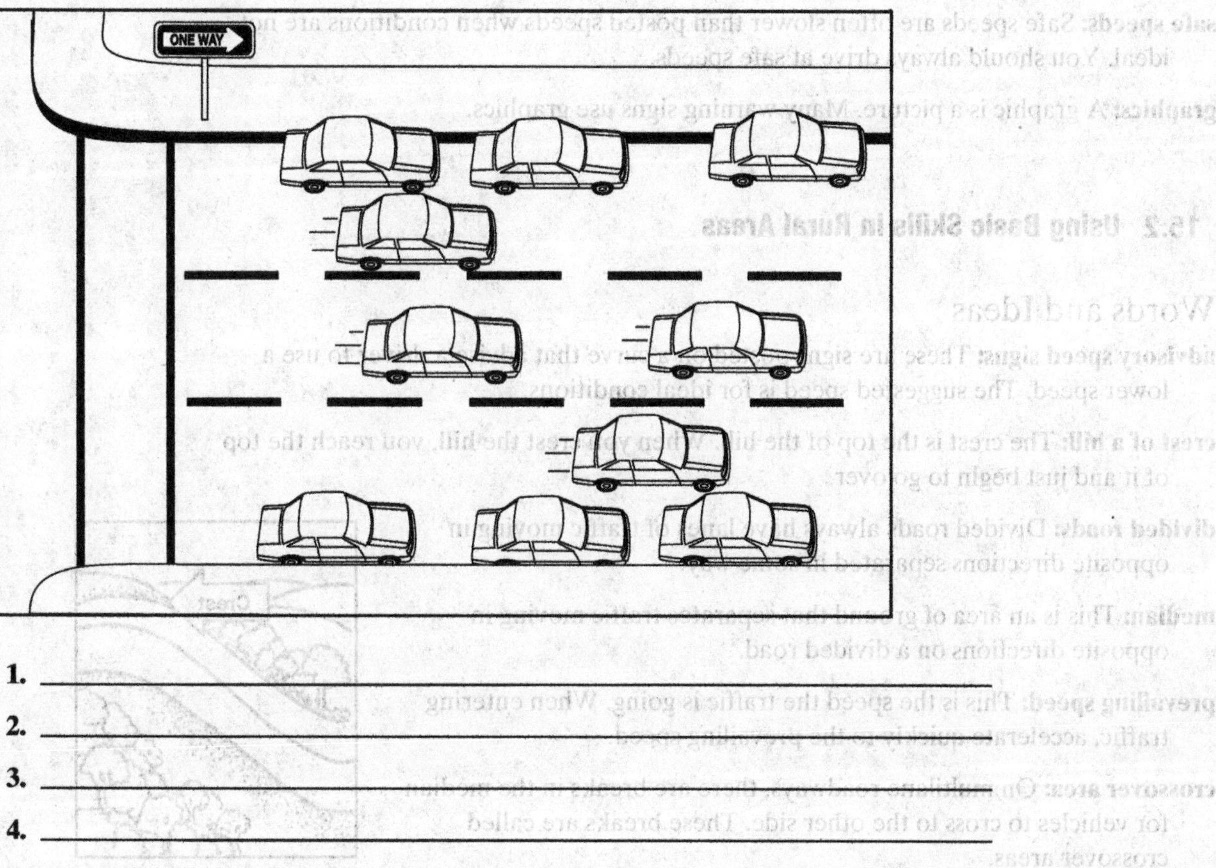

1. ______________________________
2. ______________________________
3. ______________________________
4. ______________________________

Name ______________________________ Date ______________

Learning New Words

Take a look at Chapter 15 to familiarize yourself with the topics covered. Look for all the highlighted words in **dark** print. These are the vocabulary words. Write the words on a sheet of paper, then write the meaning next to each word.

15.1 Characteristics of Rural Traffic

Words and Ideas

rural: Rural areas are in the country—farm areas and small communities.

posted speeds: Posted speeds are the maximum—highest—speeds allowed under ideal conditions.

safe speeds: Safe speeds are often slower than posted speeds when conditions are not ideal. You should always drive at safe speeds.

graphics: A graphic is a picture. Many warning signs use graphics.

15.2 Using Basic Skills in Rural Areas

Words and Ideas

advisory speed signs: These are signs posted on a curve that advise a driver to use a lower speed. The suggested speed is for ideal conditions.

crest of a hill: The crest is the top of the hill. When you crest the hill, you reach the top of it and just begin to go over.

divided roads: Divided roads always have lanes of traffic moving in opposite directions separated in some way.

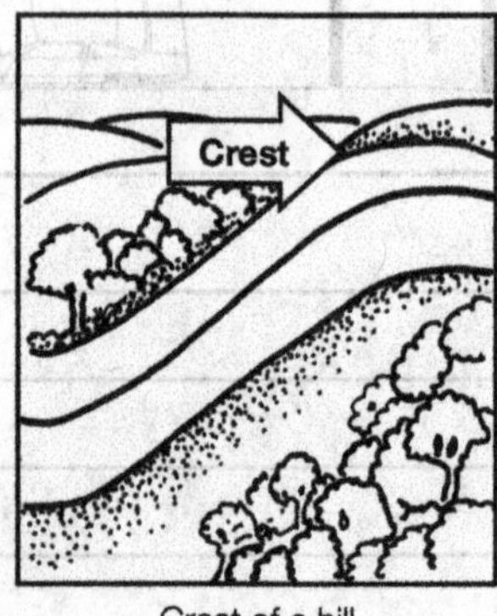

Crest of a hill

median: This is an area of ground that separates traffic moving in opposite directions on a divided road.

prevailing speed: This is the speed the traffic is going. When entering traffic, accelerate quickly to the prevailing speed.

crossover area: On multilane roadways, there are breaks in the median for vehicles to cross to the other side. These breaks are called crossover areas.

guardrail: A guardrail is a metal fence next to the road. Guardrails protect drivers at sharp curves or where the road has steep sides. If a driver loses control of the vehicle, it will hit the guardrail and stop rather than go off the road.

Name ______________________________ Date ______________

Figure It Out: When to Leave More Space

Sometimes you need to leave more space between your vehicle and the vehicle ahead. Look at the pictures below. You are driving car 1. Each picture shows a time when you need to leave more than a 3-second following distance. Choose a description from the following list, and write it under the correct picture.

being tailgated	wet pavement
on a downhill slope	following a truck

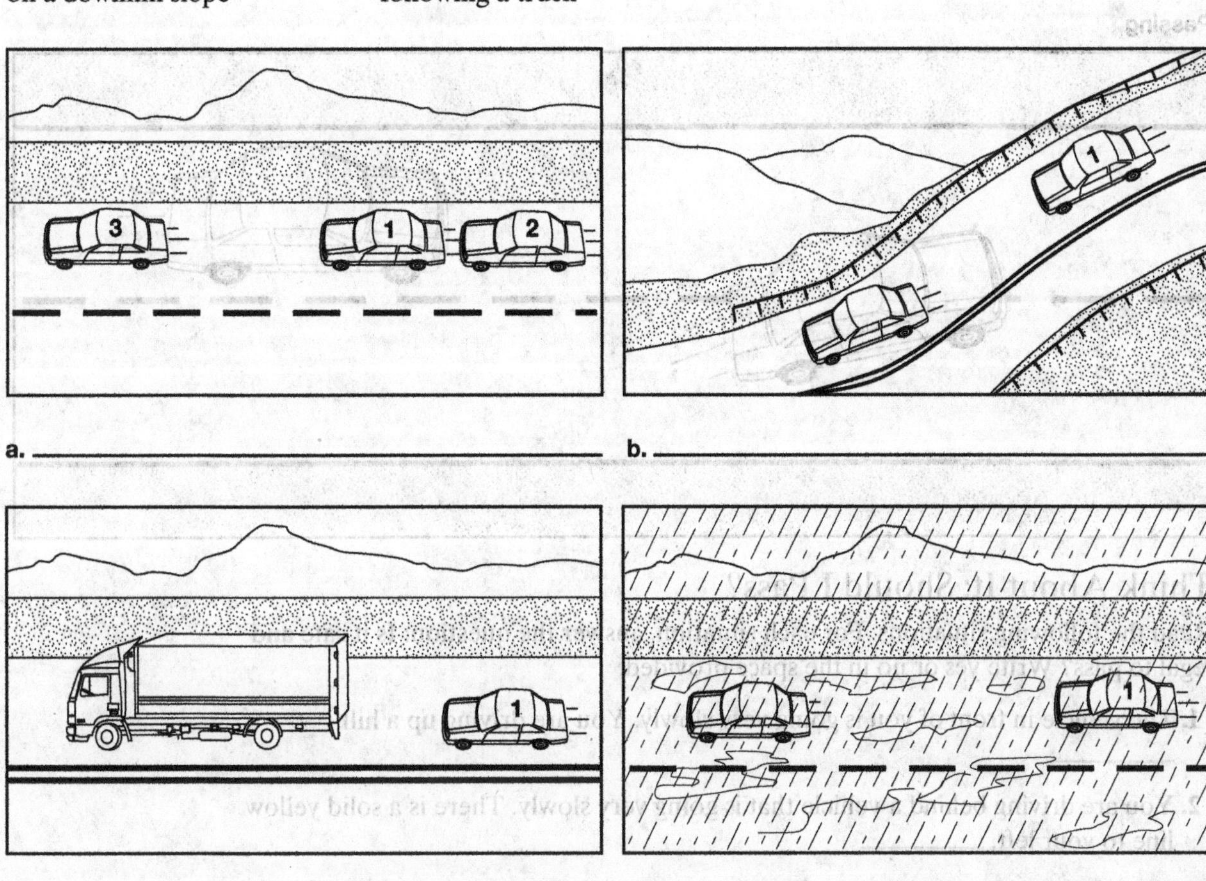

a. ______________________________ b. ______________________________

c. ______________________________ d. ______________________________

15.3 Passing and Being Passed on Rural Roads

Words and Ideas

solid yellow lines: Solid yellow lines mark no-passing zones.

prohibited: When you are prohibited from doing something, you are not allowed to do it.

Passing

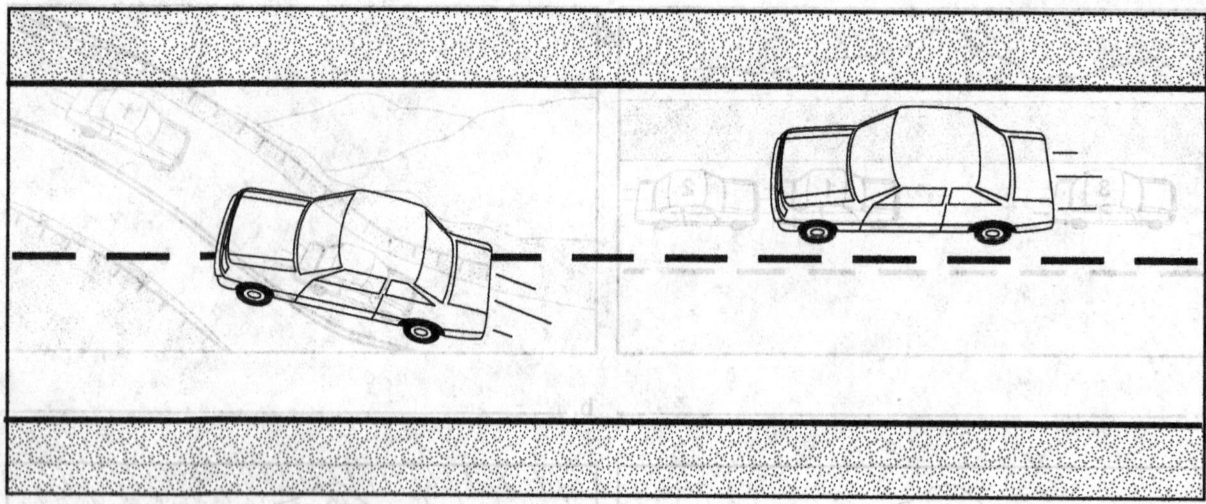

Think About It: Should I Pass?

Read the following situations. For each situation, answer the question: Is it safe and legal to pass? Write yes or no in the space provided.

1. The vehicle in front of you is going very slowly. You are driving up a hill.
____

2. You are driving behind a vehicle that is going very slowly. There is a solid yellow line to your left. __________

3. You are following a vehicle that is going very slowly. You are approaching a railroad crossing. __________

Passing on Multilane Roads Without a Median
• Check all lanes going in your direction before you pass. • Make sure no vehicle will move into your front zone and take away your path of travel. • The vehicle you are going to pass should be going slower than you are. • In general, if you pass a vehicle, you should be in the left lane.

Name ______________________________ Date ______________

15.4 Rural Situations You Might Encounter

Words and Ideas

Tractor

tractor: Tractors in rural areas are vehicles used for pulling farm machinery.

slow-moving vehicles: These are vehicles, such as tractors, that are unable to travel at highway speeds.

dart: Animals may dart—bolt or jump quickly—into your path of travel.

stragglers: Animals that stray or fall behind the group are called stragglers.

Wildlife and Farm Animals

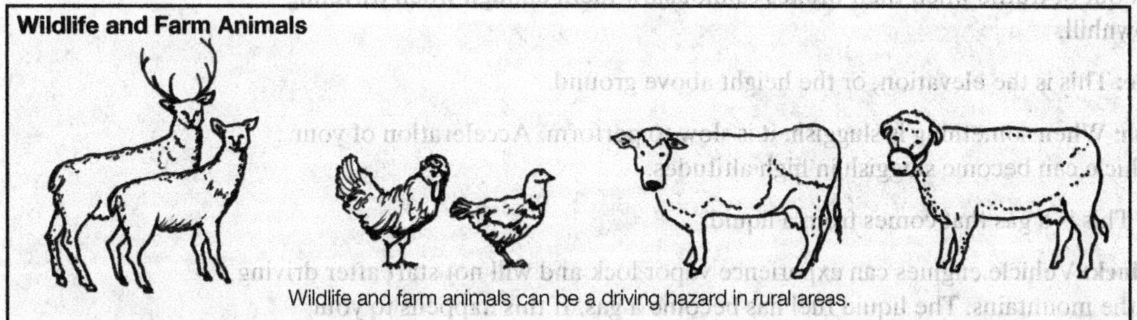
Wildlife and farm animals can be a driving hazard in rural areas.

Think About It

Read the following questions, then circle the correct answers.

1. When you see animals crossing the road, you should
   - **a.** blow your horn and drive through them.
   - **b.** stop and wait for them to pass.
   - **c.** get out of your vehicle and chase them away.

2. When approaching slow-moving vehicles, you should
   - **a.** speed up and prepare to pass.
   - **b.** slow down and prepare to pass when it is safe to do so.
   - **c.** stay behind and follow the slow-moving vehicle until it turns off the road.

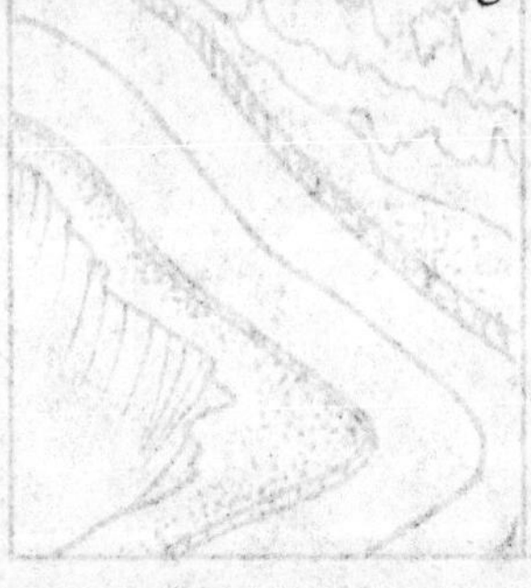

15.5 Special Driving Environments

Words and Ideas

switchbacks: These are turns in the road that bend sharply in the opposite direction.

pull-out areas: These are special lanes to the right of the main travel lane on mountain roads for slower moving vehicles.

runaway vehicle ramps: These are places on mountain roads for vehicles to safely get out of traffic when their brakes cannot slow them enough when traveling downhill.

altitude: This is the elevation, or the height above ground.

sluggish: When something is sluggish, it is slow to perform. Acceleration of your vehicle can become sluggish in high altitudes.

vapor: This is a gas that comes from a liquid.

vapor lock: Vehicle engines can experience vapor lock and will not start after driving in the mountains. The liquid fuel has become a gas. If this happens to your vehicle, allow the engine to cool before attempting to restart.

sun glare: This is strong, bright sunlight, so bright that it hurts your eyes.

sandstorms and dust storms: These are storms on the desert that lessen your driving visibility.

flash flood: A flash flood is a sudden, unexpected rush of water that is very dangerous.

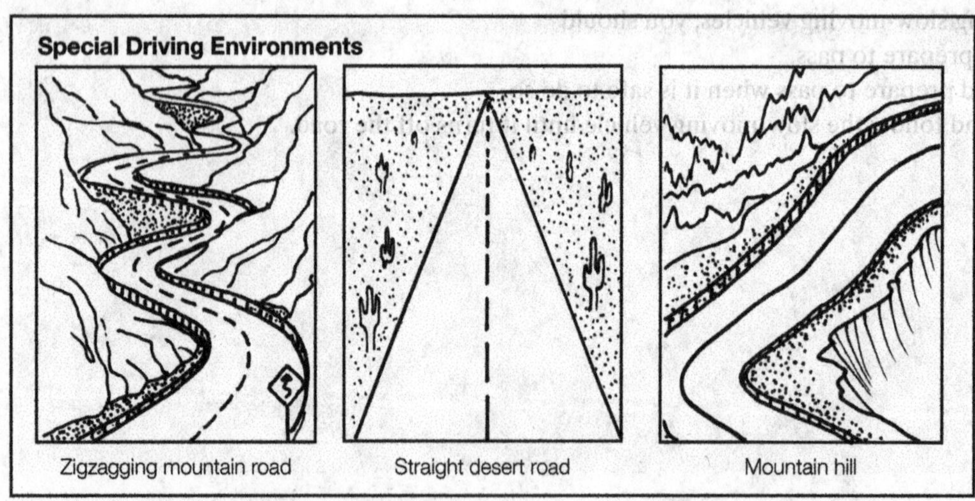

Learning New Words

Take a look at Chapter 16 to familiarize yourself with the topics covered. Look for all the highlighted words in **dark** print. These are the vocabulary words. Write the words on a sheet of paper, then write the meaning next to each word.

16.1 Classification of Highways

Words and Ideas

access: Access is a way to enter.

controlled access highway: These are highways that you can enter or leave only at an interchange. The interchanges are usually far apart.

interchange: This is the place where an expressway connects with another road. See the pictures on page 323 of *Drive Right*.

Cloverleaf interchange

non-controlled access highway: These are highways that have traffic signals and intersections where you can enter and leave.

grade elevation: Bridges and tunnels used to direct traffic over and under travel lanes are examples of grade elevation.

Interstate highway signs: These signs tell you the route number and direction of the highway.

Expressway guide sign

Name ______________________________ Date ______________

chapter 16
Companion

16.2 Entering Controlled–Access Highways

Words and Ideas

entrance ramp: This is the ramp leading onto the expressway.

acceleration lane: This is the lane that permits drivers entering an expressway to accelerate to the speed of expressway traffic.

merge: To merge is to safely move into traffic.

merging area: This is a part of roadway at the end of an acceleration lane on an expressway where vehicles join the flow of traffic.

gap: A gap is the space between two or more things. A gap in traffic is a space between vehicles.

hole in traffic: A hole in traffic is a space between groups of vehicles.

ramp meter: A ramp meter is a set of traffic signals used at an entrance ramp.

Think About It: Entering an Expressway Safely

Look at the picture below, then list the five steps you will take to enter the expressway safely.

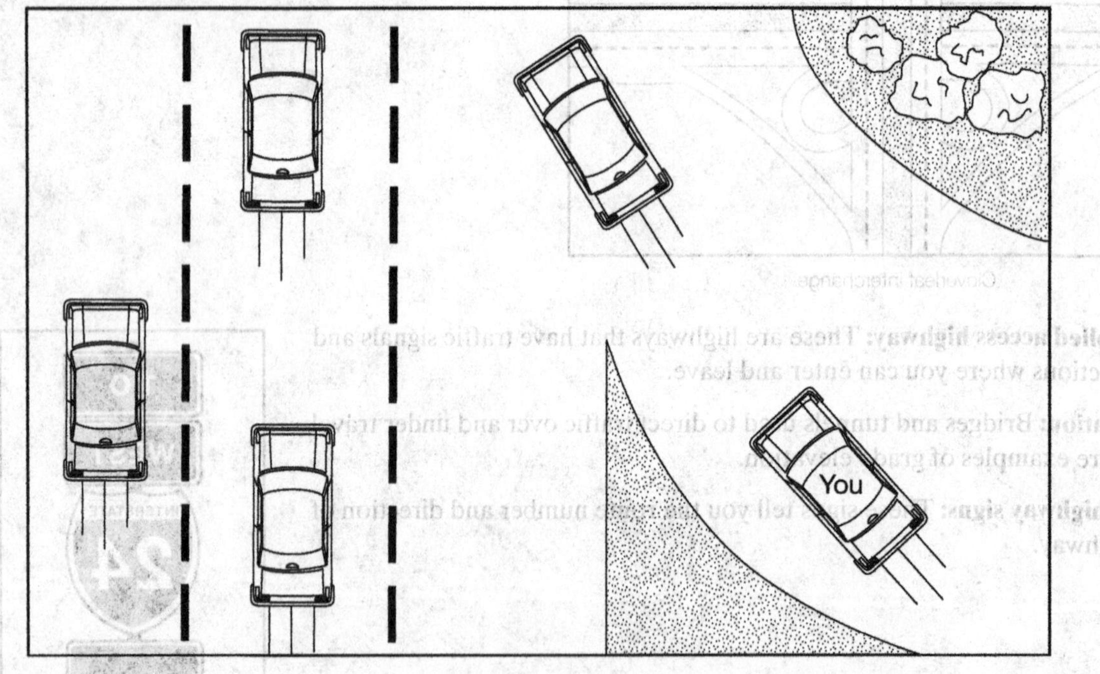

1. ______________________________
2. ______________________________
3. ______________________________
4. ______________________________
5. ______________________________

Name ______________________ Date ____________

16.3 Strategies for Driving on Highways

Words and Ideas

express lanes: Some expressways in large cities have express lanes. These lanes have fewer exits and entrances and usually have less traffic.

reversible lanes: These lanes can travel in either direction. Pay attention to traffic signals and markings to check when it is safe to use a reversible lane.

high-occupancy toll (HOT) lane: This is a high-occupancy vehicle lane that drivers without passengers can use if they pay a toll.

common speed: This is the speed used by most of the drivers on an expressway.

blend: To blend is to mix. To blend into traffic smoothly and safely means to join traffic without causing others to stop or move around you.

Think About It

Write *True* or *False* next to each of the following statements.

1. You should always signal a lane change, even when there are no cars behind you. ________
2. When traffic is backed up, you are allowed to drive on the shoulder. ________
3. During hazardous weather conditions, you may drive slower than the minimum posted speed on an expressway. ________

Name ______________________________ Date ____________

chapter 16 Companion

16.4 Exiting Controlled-Access Highways

Words and Ideas

deceleration lane: This expressway lane is used to slow your vehicle before you exit an expressway without blocking vehicles behind you.

exit ramp: This is the lane that leads off the expressway.

Figure It Out: Expressways

Label the parts of the expressway in the picture below.

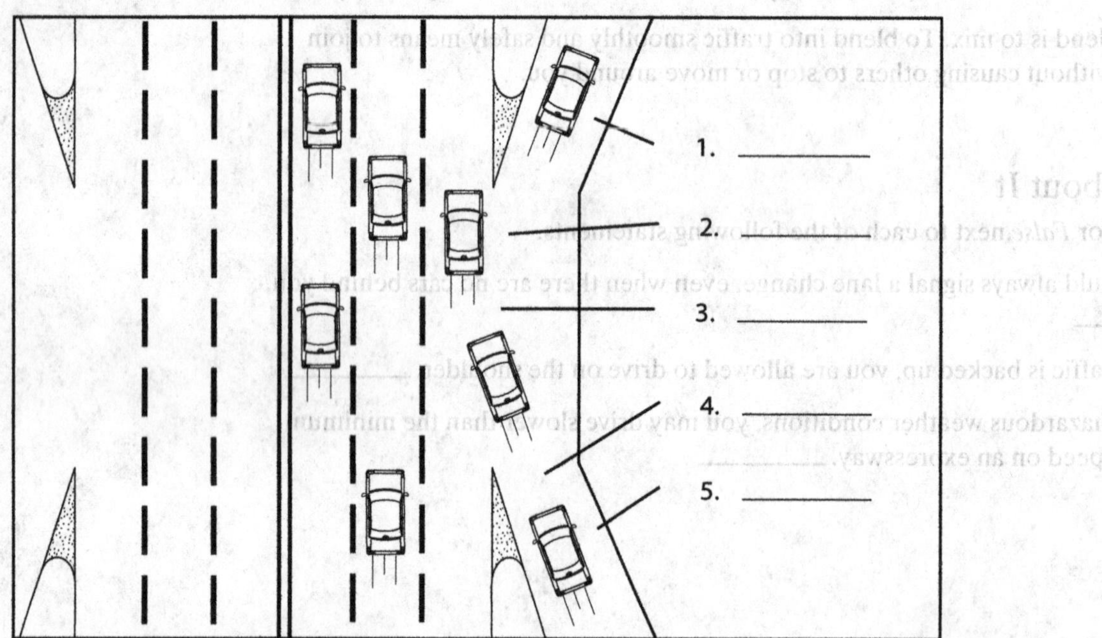

16.5 Highway Problems and Features

Words and Ideas

highway hypnosis: Being drowsy or in a trance-like condition caused by driving on a straight road with few interruptions is called highway hypnosis.

drowsy: To be drowsy is to be sleepy.

velocitation: This is not realizing that you are driving too fast as a result of driving for long periods at high speeds.

toll: A toll is the money you pay at tollbooths for using an expressway.

beltway: This is a highway that goes in a circle around a city.

spur: This is part of a highway that goes into a city.

Name ______________________________ Date ______________

Learning New Words

Take a look at Chapter 17 to familiarize yourself with the topics covered. Look for all the hightlighted words in **dark** print. These are the vocabulary words. Write the word on a sheet of paper, then write the meaning next to each word.

17.1 Buying a Vehicle

Words and Ideas

budget: This is how much money you have to spend on something.

depreciation: The decrease in the value of a vehicle over time is the depreciation.

insurance: This is a contract from an insurance company that promises to pay some or all of a vehicle owner's expenses if the vehicle is damaged or causes damage.

loan: This is money you borrow from a bank or other lender.

borrow: This is to get something from another person with the understanding that the item is to be given back. You can borrow money from a bank to buy a vehicle.

cargo: The cargo in your vehicle includes all the things you might carry, such as camping gear or sports equipment.

value: This is what something is worth.

warranty: This is a written contract that guarantees that the seller will make certain repairs for a stated period of time.

Variable Ride-Height Suspension: This is a suspension system that adjusts the height of the vehicle to be closer to, or farther from, the ground depending on conditions such as speed and terrain.

radiator: This is the part of the engine that holds the coolant, the liquid used to cool off the engine. The *radiator cap* covers the opening of the radiator.

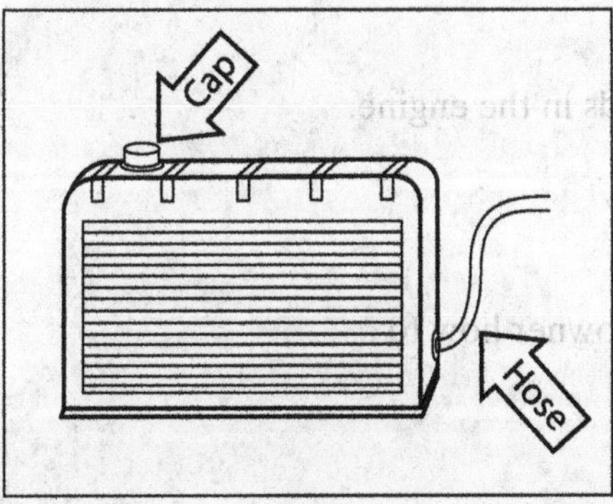

Radiator

hose: This is a rubber tube in the vehicle that is used to carry water, gas, and other liquids.

Figure It Out: Under the Hood

When you want to buy a used vehicle, you should check these items under the hood. Write the correct name for each item under its picture. Choose from the following list.

radiator   battery   fan   battery cables

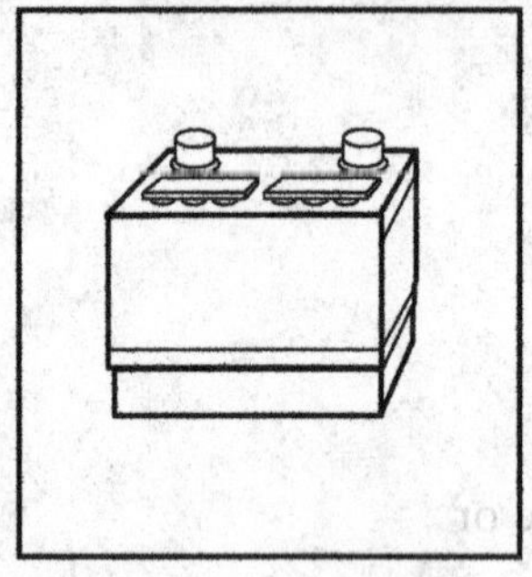

a. ______________

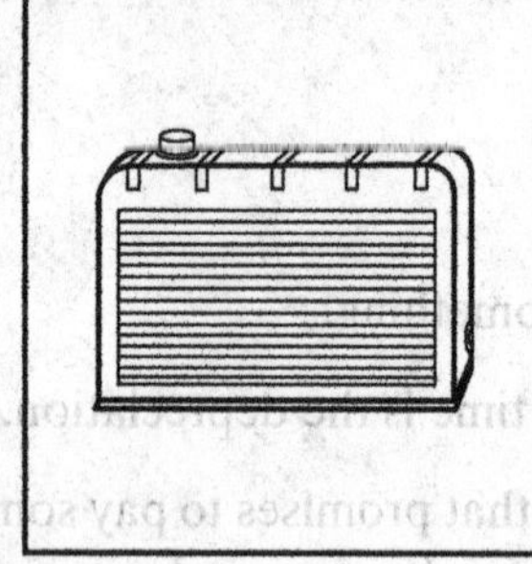

b. ______________

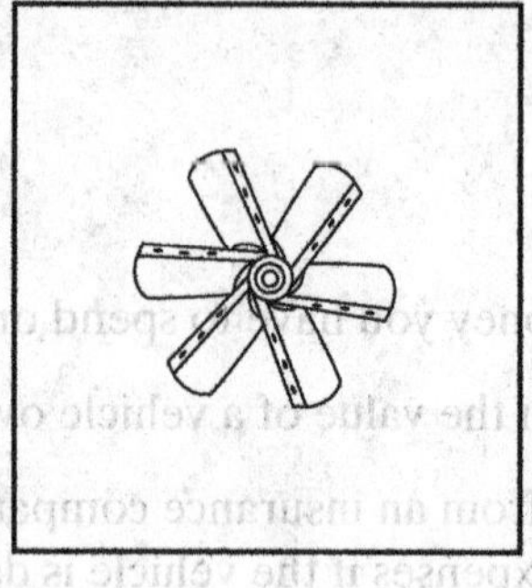

c. ______________

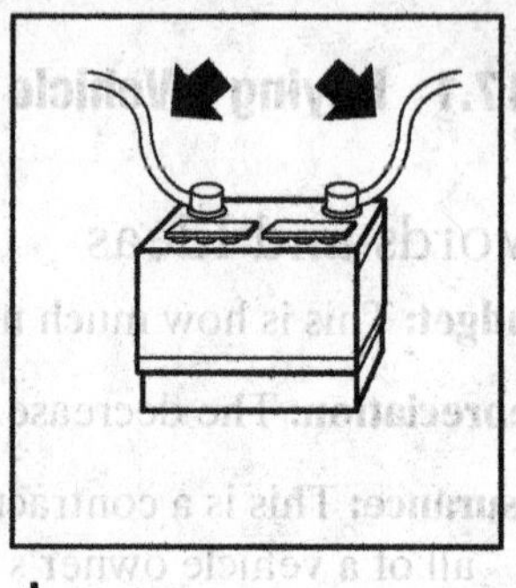

d. ______________

17.2 Preventive Maintenance

Words and Ideas

routine: Routine means regular and ordinary. Routine checks of your vehicle involve checking things in a regular way each time you drive.

maintain: This means to keep in good repair, to take care of.

preventive maintenance: Preventive maintenance is regular care and attention to your vehicle to keep it working well.

electronic control module: This is a computer that controls how well the engine works.

carburetor: This is an engine part that mixes air and gasoline and sends it as a mist for combustion in the engine cylinders.

catalytic converter: This is the part of a vehicle's emission system that converts harmful gases into less harmful gases and water.

muffler: This is a device that reduces the noise from combustion sounds in the engine.

lubricate: To lubricate something is to make it smooth and slippery.

coolant: Coolant is a liquid used to take heat away from the engine.

owner's manual: This is the book that comes with a vehicle to tell the owner how to maintain the vehicle and how everything on the vehicle works.

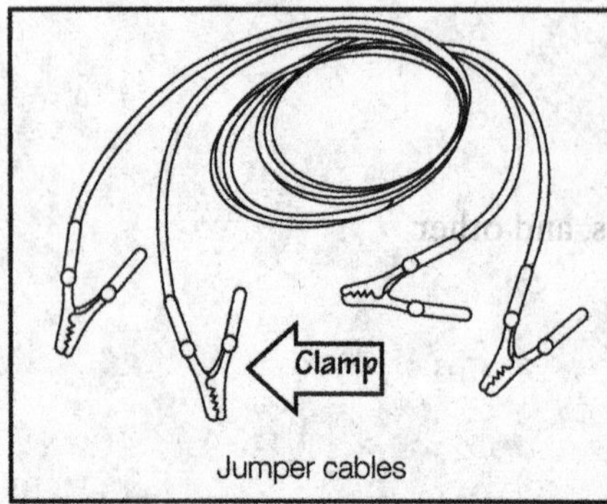

Jumper cables

power steering: This system uses a hydraulic pump and fluid to make steering easier.

disk brake: This is part of the brake system that works as fluid pressure forces the brake shoes against the hollow cylinder drum inside the wheel.

parking brake: This is a separate braking system with a lever or special pedal used to hold a parked car in place.

annual: This means yearly. Your annual operating costs for your vehicle are all the costs for one year.

battery: A charged battery is one that works; a charged battery gives electricity.

dead battery: A dead battery does not give electricity; a dead battery is one that does not work.

cable: This is a tube that carries wires. A battery cable sends electrical current through wires to start your vehicle.

jump start: This is to start a battery with jumper cables. When you jump start a battery, you charge a dead vehicle battery by connecting it to a charged vehicle battery and starting the first vehicle with the charged battery.

jumper cables: These are electrical cables used to jump start dead vehicle batteries.

Think About It

Write your answers to the following questions in the space provided.

1. Find the oil pressure warning light in your vehicle. What does it mean when this light comes on? ______________________________

____

2. Find the brake warning light in your vehicle. What does it mean when this light comes on? ______________________________

____

____

Name ______________________ Date ______________

17.3 Fuel-Efficiency, Recycling, and Security Systems

Words and Ideas

fuel-efficient: A fuel-efficient car functions using the least amount of fuel possible.

gas mileage: The gas mileage is the number of miles a vehicle travels for each gallon of gas it uses (miles per gallon). Smaller vehicles usually get better gas mileage than larger vehicles.

calculate: To calculate is to figure. When calculating miles per gallon, you are figuring how many miles your vehicle goes on a gallon of gas.

odometer: This tells the number of miles a vehicle has traveled.

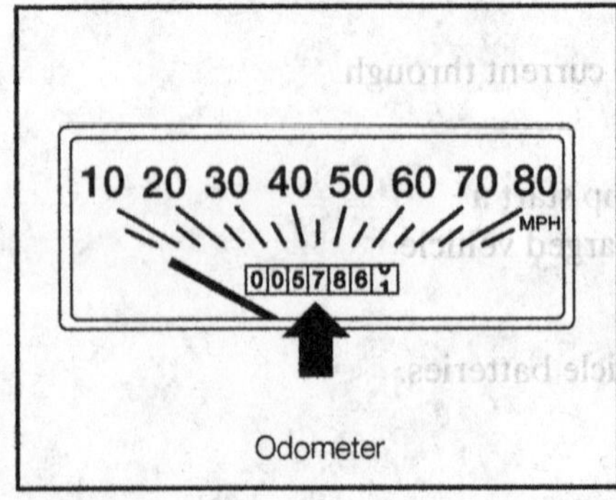

alternative fuel: Alternative fuels are fuels that are not made from petroleum.

recycle: To recycle is to use again.

transmission: This is a mechanism in a vehicle that carries power from the engine to the drive wheels.

Figure It Out: Fuel Consumption

Look at pictures a and b. Then circle the best answer.

1. Which car is more fuel efficient? a b
2. Which car consumes more fuel? a b
3. Which car costs less to drive 300 miles? a b

Name ________________ Date ________

Learning New Words

Take a look at Chapter 18 to familiarize yourself with the topics covered. Look for all the highlighted words in **dark** print. These are the vocabulary words. Write the word on a sheet of paper, then write the meaning next to each word.

18.1 Environmental Concerns

Words and Ideas

pollution: This is wasteful material or fumes that harm the air we breathe and the land on which we live.

hazardous substances: These are substances that are harmful to human beings.

dispose: This means to throw away or get rid of.

ozone layer: The ozone layer is a layer of gas high in the sky. It shields Earth from the sun's harmful ultraviolet rays.

Ozone layer

emits: This means to give out or to send out. Your vehicle emits gases.

emissions: Emissions are something sent out into the air. The emissions that come from your vehicle's exhaust pipe are made of gases that can harm the environment.

On-Board Diagnostic (OBD) system: This is a computer system inside a vehicle that keeps track of whether the vehicle's parts are working properly.

public transportation: this is a way to move large numbers of people together from place to place. Buses, trains, and transit systems are used for mass transportation.

carpooling: When several people share a ride to one or more places in one car, it is called a carpool.

18.2 Local Travel

Words and Ideas

destination: Your destination is where you are going; the end of your trip.

smooth: Smooth driving is driving that is easy and relaxed.

routine check: A routine check takes place when you check something out of habit whenever you do something else. One example is checking your tire pressure every time you fill your vehicle's fuel tank.

18.3 Long-Distance Travel

Words and Ideas

navigation: Navigation is the process of finding a way to your destination.

Global Positioning System: This is a system of satellites orbiting Earth. It is used by navigation systems, called GPS receivers, to tell where a vehicle is.

map: A map is a drawing of roadways, cities, towns, and other areas of interest for a state or country. You can use a map to help you plan a route to take from one point to another.

legend: This is a chart that explains the markings and symbols used on a map.

mileage scale: This is a chart on a map that shows the distance between two cities.

coordinates: Coordinates on a map are letters on one side and numbers on another side that help you locate a place on the map.

18.4 Special Vehicles

Words and Ideas

recreational vehicle: These are large vehicles used mainly for pleasure and travel. Examples are a van, motor home, camper, travel trailer, pickup truck, or sport utility vehicle.

trailer hitch: This is something used to attach a trailer to a car or truck.

safety chain: This is a chain connecting a trailer to a vehicle as a backup link in case the trailer hitch fails.

Recreational Vehicles

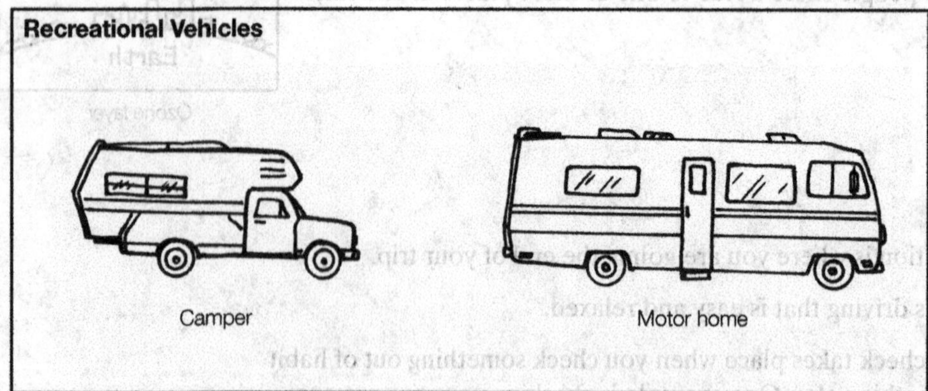

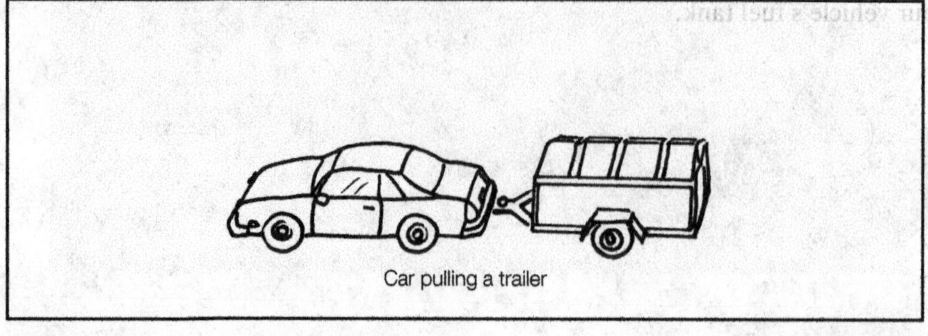

CHAPTER 1

Page 6 Think About It

1. multilane expressway
2. dirt road, road with steep grade, road with sharp turns

Page 9 Think About It

1. a
2. b
3. b
4. b

Page 10 Think About It

1. True
2. True
3. False

CHAPTER 2

Page 13 Think About It

1. basic speed law
2. minimum speed limit
3. advisory speed limit

Page 14 Think About It

1. school zone sign
2. school crossing sign
3. no passing sign
4. construction sign
5. railroad advance-warning sign

Page 15 Think About It

1. b
2. b
3. a

Page 15 Figure It Out: Find the Picture

1. 27
2. 29
3. 28
4. 30

CHAPTER 3

Page 19 Think About It

1. full
2. empty
3. almost full
4. 9
5. 360

Page 25 Double Trouble

a. part of a vehicle that turns engine speed into power to turn the wheels
b. a pedal that helps you shift gears in a manual transmission vehicle

CHAPTER 4

Page 26 and 27 Figure It Out: Steering Straight Backward

1. Place your foot firmly on the brake, and shift into reverse.
2. Use a target to aim the car toward. Look over your right shoulder to see your targeting path.
3. Check all three mirrors to supplement looking over your shoulder.
4. Travel no faster than a crawl by slightly releasing brake-pedal pressure.

Page 27 Think About It

By keeping your foot over the brake pedal, you will be able to slow down or stop quickly if you begin swerving or something appears in your path of travel.

Page 31 Think About It

1. a and b
2. a
3. b and c

CHAPTER 5

Page 32 Think About It: Habits

1. bad habit
2. good habit
3. bad habit
4. good habit

Page 33 Think About It: The IPDE Process

There are many ways to answer this exercise. Here is an example.

1. Identify open and closed zones, clues, other users, roadway conditions, and traffic controls.
2. Predict actions of other users, change of direction, points of conflict, and consequences.
3. Decide what action to take (to change speed, change direction, or communicate).
4. Execute your decision (control speed, steer, communicate, or combine actions).

Page 34 Think About It

1. closed front zone
2. closed right-front zone
3. closed rear zone

Page 36 Think About It: Driving Detective

1 and 3

Page 37 Figure It Out: Hazards

1. The dog might run across the street after the cat.
2. The ball might roll into the street and the boy might run after it.
3. The car in the driveway might pull out in front of me.

Page 38 Think About It: Predictions

1. The lamp is going to fall.
2. The girl is going to run into the tree.
3. The cat is going to eat the fish.

Page 40 Think About It

1. False
2. True
3. False

Page 40 Think About It: Using the IPDE Process

I identify deer in the road. I predict that they might run into my path of travel. I decide to slow down. I apply the brake.

CHAPTER 6

Page 42 Think About It: Feelings and Emotions

1. excitement
2. anger
3. depression
4. heated discussion

Page 45 Think About It

1. There is less light.
2. Do not look directly at bright lights; wear sunglasses; and use your vehicle's sun visor.

CHAPTER 7

Page 47 Figure It Out: Fatal Crashes

1. c
2. a

Page 48 Think About It

1. False
2. False
3. False

CHAPTER 8

Page 52 Think About It

Answers can vary. Accept any four of the following responses.
1. Avoid using a cell phone.
2. Set volume and radio channels before driving.
3. Secure loose objects or animals before driving.
4. Avoid eating or drinking while driving.
5. Set rules for passengers.

Page 53 Think About It: Gawking and Rubbernecking

Answers can vary. Students may point out that motorists gawking at a crash often cause more traffic congestion than the crash itself. They may also say that this sort of gawking is likely to cause rear-end collisions. Similar issues exist with rubbernecking.

Page 53 Think About It

1. False
2. True
3. True
4. False
5. True

CHAPTER 9

Page 56 Think About It: Energy of Motion

1. b
2. b
3. a

Page 57 Think About It

a; b; d; e; f

Page 58 Think About It

a; b; c; d; f

Page 59 Double Trouble

a. 1
b. 1
c. 2
d. 2
e. 2

Page 62 Think About It

1. False
2. True
3. False
4. True
5. False

CHAPTER 10

Page 63 Figure It Out: Intersections

a. street signs, parked cars on cross street
b. fences, mailbox

Page 67 Think About It: Uncontrolled Intersections

1. b
2. a
3. b

Page 69 Think About It

1. a
2. b

Page 69 Think About It

1. True
2. False
3. True
4. True

CHAPTER 11

Page 71 Figure It Out: Bicycle Hazards

1. The bicyclist is wearing headphones and is not wearing a helmet.
2. A car door is open in the cyclist's path.
3. A car is tailgating the cyclist.
4. There is a pothole in the cyclist's path.

Page 72 Think About It

a. 2
b. 3
c. 4
d. 1
e. 5

Page 73 Think About It

1. False
2. False
3. False
4. True

CHAPTER 12

Page 75 Figure It Out

1. b
2. a

Page 75 Think About It

1. False
2. True

Page 78 Figure It Out

Answers will vary, but most students will answer "no" to all questions.

Page 80 Think About It

1. b
2. b
3. b
4. b

Page 80 Figure It Out

1. glare ice
2. concrete
3. 40 feet

Page 80 Think About It

1. a
2. b

Page 81 Think About It

1. True
2. False
3. True
4. False
5. False

CHAPTER 13

Page 84 Figure It Out: Brake Failure

1. 4
2. 2
3. 1
4. 3

Page 84 Figure It Out: Emergencies

1. d
2. b
3. a
4. c

Page 85 Think About It

1. b
2. a
3. b

Page 86 Think About It

1. to keep control of the vehicle and to avoid tire damage
2. Try to open a door to exit.

Page 87 Figure It Out

1. stop and help any victims
2. name, address, driver's license number, license plate number, insurance company name

Page 87 Think About It

Head-on collisions cause the most serious injuries because the force of impact between the two cars is the highest.

Page 88 Figure It Out: Insuring a Vehicle

Cross out: interest, warranty, loan, depreciation

CHAPTER 14

Page 90 Figure It Out: Driving Distractions

All items distract you from driving safely.

Page 91 Think About It

1. a
2. b
3. both a and b

Page 91 Think About It

1. False; you should increase your following distance.
2. True
3. False; you should slow down to maintain the correct following distance from the vehicle ahead of you.

Page 92 Think About It

1. yes
2. no
3. yes
4. yes

Page 92 Think About It: Riding Your Brake

Riding your brakes wears out the brakes faster. Your brake lights stay on, and the drivers behind you think you are going to slow down or stop.

Page 93 Figure It Out: One-Way Streets

1. one-way sign
2. All the cars are parked in the same direction.
3. Traffic in all three lanes is moving in the same direction.
4. Broken white lines are used as lane lines for all lanes.

CHAPTER 15

Page 95 Figure It Out: When to Leave More Space

a. being tailgated
b. on a downhill slope
c. following a truck
d. wet pavement

Page 96 Think About It: Should I Pass?

1. No
2. No
3. No

Page 97 Think About It

1. b
2. b

CHAPTER 16

Page 100 Think About It: Entering an Expressway Safely

1. Make sure this is the entrance I want.
2. Once on the ramp, check my front and rear zones. Signal my intention, glance at the left outside rearview mirror, glance over my left shoulder, and look for the gap in traffic.
3. Increase my speed in the acceleration lane. Keep checking the gap to make sure it is safe to merge.
4. Decide which vehicle to follow when merging. Enter the merging area, adjust my speed to match the flow of traffic, and position my vehicle at a safe interval behind the vehicle I plan to follow. Merge smoothly.
5. Once I'm on the expressway, cancel the signal and keep a safe space cushion around my vehicle.

Page 101 Think About It

1. True
2. False
3. True

Page 102 Figure It Out: Expressways

1. exit ramp
2. deceleration lane
3. merging area
4. acceleration lane
5. entrance ramp

CHAPTER 17

Page 104 Figure It Out: Under the Hood

1. battery
2. radiator
3. fan
4. battery cables

Page 105 Think About It

1. Oil pressure in the engine is low. This can be very harmful to the engine.
2. There is a leak in the brake system, so the brakes are not working the way they should.

Page 106 Figure It Out: Fuel Consumption

1. b
2. a
3. b

A

ability, 32
absorption rate, 47
abstain, 46
abuse, 46
accelerate, 22, 39
acceleration lane, 100
accelerator, 22
access, 99
accessory, 24
active railroad crossing, 68
active restraint device, 62
adjust, 23
administer, 86
adverse weather, 74
advisory speed limits, 13
advisory speed signs, 94
aggressive, 41
aid, 86
air bag, 20, 62
air pocket, 85
alcoholism, 47
alert, 72
alignment, 82
allergic, 52
alley, 70
alternative fuel, 106
alternator warning light, 19
altitude, 98
amphetamines, 48
ample 90
analyze, 32
anesthetic, 46
angle parking, 30
annual, 105
anticipate, 72
antihistamine, 48
antilock braking system, 20
anxiety, 41
assess, 41
assumptions or expectations, 41
attention, 89
auditory, 51
avoid, 29

B

backing, 26
backlog, 53
bald tire, 57
bank, 59
banked curve, 58
basic speed law, 13
battery, 19, 105
beltway, 102
biomechanical, 51
black ice, 79
blast of wind, 81
blend, 101
blind intersection, 93
blind-spot areas, 22
blizzard, 78
blood alcohol concentration (BAC), 47
blowout, 57, 82
bodily-injury insurance, 88
borrow, 103
brake fade, 83
brake lights, 20
brake warning light, 83
braking distance, 60
brief, 85
budget, 103
bumper, 31
business districts, 70

C

cable, 105
calculate, 106
capabilities, 52
carbon monoxide, 45
carburetor, 104
cargo, 103
carpool, 92, 107
carpooling, 92, 107
catalytic converter, 104
cellular phone, 89
center of gravity, 58
central nervous system, 46
central vision, 36
check, 12
chronic illness, 45
circulate, 18
claims, 88
closed zone, 34
clutch, 25
clutch pedal, 22
cognitive, 51
collision, 8
collision insurance, 88
color coded, 17

color-blindness, 44
combat, 45
combination, 79
combine actions, 39
commitment, 53
common speed, 101
compact spare, 83
compensate, 45
complexity, 89
comprehensive insurance, 88
compromise space, 39
conflict, 32
congested, 93
consent, 49
construction zone, 13
consume, 49
control, 54
controlled access highway, 99
controlled braking, 80
controlled intersection, 65
controlled steering, 24
convex, 26
conviction, 49
coolant, 18, 104
coordinates, 108
courteous driver, 7
cover the brake, 92
crawl, 26
crest of a hill, 94
critical clues, 32
crosswinds, 81
crossbuck, 68
crossing gates, 68
crossing guard, 13
crossover area, 94
crosswalk, 12
crucial, 72
cruise control, 20
cruise, 20
curve, 58

D

dart, 97
dead battery, 105
decelerate, 39
deceleration lane, 102
decide, 7, 39
deductible, 88
delayed green light, 66
dense, 89
depreciation, 103
depressant, 48
depression, 41
depth perception, 44
designated driver, 47
destination, 107
diagonally, 30
directional arrows, 16
disability, 45
disabled, 39
disk brake, 105
dispose, 107
disruptive, 52
distort, 46
distract, 41
distracted driving, 51
distraction, 51, 89
divided roads, 94
double, 56
drained, 19
driver errors, 85
driver inattention, 51
driver's license, 6
driving task, 7
driving under the influence (DUI), 49
driving while intoxicated (DWI), 49
drop off, 85
drowsy, 102

E

efficient, 9
electronic control module, 104
emergency vehicles, 64, 75
emissions, 107
emits, 107
emotion, 41
endanger, 42
energy of motion, 54
entrance ramp, 100
equalize, 85
erratic, 46
euphoria, 46
evaluate, 38
excessive, 47
execute, 7, 39
exhaust pipe, 81
exit ramp, 102
experience, 38
express lanes, 101
extreme, 52

F

fatally injured, 46
fatigue, 41, 51
field of vision, 36, 43
field sobriety test, 49
financial responsibility law, 88
fine, 49
fire extinguisher, 84
fire hydrants, 17
fishtail, 79
fishtailing, 82
fixate, 36, 46
fixed, 25
fixed costs, 8
flares, 84
flash flood, 98
flash your brake lights, 90
flashing signal, 15
flick your headlights, 77
following distance, 90
force, 54
force of impact, 61
forward vision, 84
four times, 56
fresh green light, 65
friction, 57
fringe vision, 44
front-window defroster, 77
fuel consumption, 9
fuel-efficient, 9, 106
full, 12
full-privilege license stage, 10
fumes, 45

G

gap, 64, 100
gas mileage, 106
gauge, 18
gawking, 53
generate, 19
gestures, 42
glare, 44, 77
glare recovery time, 44
glare resistance, 44
Global Positioning System, 108
goggles, 73
grade, 85
grade elevation, 99
graduated driver licensing program, 10
graphics, 94
gravel, 37
gravity, 54
groove, 57
ground viewing, 36
guardrail, 94
guide sign, 11

H

habit, 32, 42
hallucinogens, 48
hand signals, 28
hand throttle, 71
handicapped parking, 17
hand-operated brakes, 71
hand-over-hand steering, 25
hands-free technology, 52
hand-to-hand steering, 25
hazardous substances, 107
hazards, 32
headphones, 71
head restraints, 22
head-on collision, 78, 86
helmet, 73
High-Occupancy Vehicle (HOV) lanes, 92
high-occupancy toll (HOT) lane, 101
high-beam headlights, 20, 77
highway hypnosis, 102
highway transportation system (HTS), 5
hole in traffic, 100
hydroplaning, 57, 79

I

ideal, 13
identify, 7, 32
ignition switch, 24
illegal *per se* laws, 49
illuminate, 84
impact, 61
impaired, 46
implied consent law, 49
indicator lights, 18
industrial smoke, 78
inertia, 54
informative, 53
inhibitions, 46
injury, injuries, 22
inspect, 23
instrument panel, 18
insurance, 103

interchange, 99
intermediate license stage, 10
international symbols, 14
intersection, 11
Interstate highway signs, 99
intervene, 42
intoxication, 47
intoxilyzer, 49
IPDE Process, 7
irresponsible, 41

J

jaywalk, 70
joining traffic, 64
judgment, 38
jump start, 105
jumper cables, 105

L

lane changes, 28
lane signal, 16
learner's permit stage, 10
legal, 70
legend, 108
lever, 20
liability insurance, 88
line of sight, 34
load, 59
loan, 103
location, 67
locking your wheels, 80
low-beam headlights, 77
low-risk driving, 8
low-speed vehicles (LSVs), 76
lubricate, 104
luxury, 52

M

maintain, 104
major, 72
malfunction, 82
maneuver, 29
manslaughter, 49
manual transmission, 25
map, 108
marbles, 79
marijuana, 48
maximum, 13
median, 94
medical-payment insurance, 88
mental skills, 46
merge, 100
merging area, 100
midblock, 29
mileage scale, 108
minimize, 86
minimize a hazard, 39
minimum, 13
moisture, 77
momentum, 54
moped, 71
moral, 70
moral and legal obligation, 70
motorcyclist, 72
muffler, 104
multimedia, 52
murder, 49

N

natural laws, 54
nausea, 45
navigation, 108
navigational, 52
neighborhood electric vehicles (NEVs), 76
night blindness, 44
no-fault insurance, 88
non-controlled access highway, 99
note, 86
notify, 87
no zones, 76
nystagmus, 49

O

obligation, 70
obstruction, 26
odometer, 18, 106
odorless, 45
offense, 86
offset position, 74
oil marks, 23
On-Board Diagnostic (OBD) system, 107
oncoming traffic, 12
one-way street, 93
open zone, 34
operating costs, 8
opportunities, 52
orderly, 35
orderly visual search pattern, 35

ordinance, 52
overdriving headlights, 77
overhead, 37
overheats, 84
overinflation, 57
overpasses, 79
oversteer situation, 79
overtake, 92
over-the-counter (OTC) medicine, 48
owner's manual, 104
oxidized, 47
ozone layer, 107

P

parallel, 31
parallel parking, 31
paramedics, 86
park, 30
parking brake, 83, 105
passive railroad crossing, 68
passive restraint device, 62
path of travel, 34
pedal, 22
pedestrian signal, 16
pedestrians, 70
peer education, 50
peer influence, 50
peer pressure, 41, 50
penalty, penalties, 49
perceive, 59
perception distance, 60
perception time, 60
perimeter, 53
peripheral vision, 36
perpendicular parking, 30
personal reference points, 30
pharmacist, 48
physical abilities, 46
physical, 45
pitch, 58
point of no return, 63
policy, 88
pollution, 107
posted speeds, 94
potential, 42, 53
potholes, 85
power lines, 63
power steering, 105
predict, 7, 32
premium, 88
prescription, 48
prescription medicine, 48
pressure, 18
prevailing speed, 94
preventive maintenance, 104
prison term, 49
procedure, 23
proceed, 12
prohibited, 96
projectile, 52
promptly, 87
proof, 47
proof of financial responsibility, 87
property-damage insurance, 88
proportional, 61
protect, 8
protected left turn, 65
protective gear, 73
public transportation, 107
pull-out areas, 98
puncture, 57

R

racing the engine, 81
radiator, 103
rage, 41
railroad crossing, 14
ramp meter, 100
rate, 46
react, 41
reaction distance, 60
reaction time, 60
reading traffic situations, 32
rear-end collision, 86
rear defogger, 77
reckless, 41
recreational vehicle, 108
recycle, 106
reduced visibility, 77
re-enter, 29
reference point, 30
reflective markers, 17
reflective tape, 71
reflex, 46
refrain, 41
regulate, 6
regulatory sign, 11
release, 20
repair, 36
reserved, 17

residential areas, 70
responsibility, 8
restraint device, 62
restriction, 34
restrictions, 71
revenge, 41
reversible lanes, 101
revocation, 49
ride the brake, 92
right angle, 30
right of way, 11, 64
right-turn-on-red, 16
risk, 5
risk factors, 32
roadway markings, 17
roadway surface, 37
roadway users, 5
rocking a vehicle, 79
route, 14
roundabout, 69
routine, 104
routine check, 107
rubbernecking, 53
rumble strips, 17
runaway vehicle ramps, 98
rural, 94
rush hour, 16

S

safe speeds, 94
safe-driving memory bank, 38
safety chain, 108
safety stop, 63
sandstorms and dust storms, 98
scald, 81
scanning, 36
school zone, 13
scooter, 72
searching ranges, 36
seldom, 84
selective, 40
selective seeing, 36
semi-automatic transmission, 25
semi-trailer, 76
separate the hazards, 39
share, 72
shared left-turn lane, 17
shift indicator, 20
shoulder, 84
side effect, 45
side-impact collision, 86
sirens, 75
skid, 79
skidding, 37
skills, 7
sleet, 79
sliding, 37
slow-moving vehicles, 97
sluggish, 98
slush, 78
smoke residue, 45
smooth, 107
snowplows, 75
solid yellow lines, 96
sorrow, 41
space cushion, 39
spare tire, 83
speed, 38
speed limit signs, 13
speed smear, 45
spin, 79
spur, 102
square, 59
square of a number, 56
squeeze, 79
stability, 58, 72
stable, 59
stale green light, 65
stall, 25
stalled, 81
standard reference point, 30
standing water, 79
steer, 39
stimulant, 48
STOP sign, 12
stragglers, 97
straight, 26
straighten, 30
stressful, 41
substantial, 52
sun glare, 98
sun visor, 77
suspension, 49
swerve, 71, 85
switchbacks, 98
synergistic effect, 48

T

tailgate, tailgater, 90
tank, 18

tape, 71
target, 25
target area, 34
temperature, 57
3-second following distance, 90
through lane, 37
through street, 65
tire chains, 79
toll, 102
tornado, 81
total stopping distance, 59
traction, 38, 57
tractor, 97
tractor-trailer, 76
traffic control officer, 16
traffic controls, 37
traffic density, 89
traffic jams, 45
traffic signal, 15
trailer, 76
trailer hitch, 108
transmission, 25, 106
tread, 57
tunnel vision, 43
turnabout, 29

U

unbalanced wheels, 82
uncontrolled intersections, 66
underage, 46
underinflation, 57
underinsured motorist insurance, 88
understeer situation, 79
unevenly, 82
uninsured motorist insurance, 88
unprotected left turn, 65
update, 67
upholstery, 84
U-turn, 29

V

value, 103
vapor, 98
vapor lock, 98
Variable Ride-Height Suspension, 103
vehicle, 6
vehicle balance, 58
velocitation, 102
vigorously enforced, 46
visible, 74
visual, 35, 51
visual acuity, 43
vulnerable, 70

W

warning sign, 11
warranty, 103
wear, 82
whiplash, 22
wind gust, 76
wind-driven snow, 78
windshield wipers, 78
witness, 86

Y

yield, 11, 64

Z

zero tolerance law, 49
zone, 34
Zone Control System, 8, 34